ISBN-13: 978-1-7338016-8-3

This book is dedicated to my husband Tony.

You're solid proof I wasn't 100% bad in all my past lives.


And to my parents Jim and Jenny Seibert:

There is nothing as important as parents who believe in
their children, and grandchildren, and support their
dreams (and throw amazing weddings!).

# Chapters

Introduction

## Physical

Chapter 1: Let's Get Physical

Chapter 2: What's Your Kryptonite?

Chapter 3: Memories Light the Corners of My Mind

Chapter 4: After the Holidays

Chapter 5: The Junk Drawer

## Mental

Chapter 6: Past, Present or Future?

Chapter 7: The Just Becauses

Chapter 8: When Life Throws a Curveball

Chapter 9: Do Something Differently

Chapter 10: Unplugging

## Emotional

Chapter 11: Better Be Good to Me

Chapter 12: When Life Knocks You Down

Chapter 13: What's Your Baggage?

Chapter 14: The Green-Eyed Monster

Chapter 15: Feel Your Feelings

## Spiritual

Chapter 16: Do You

Chapter 17: Give Thanks

Chapter 18: Simplify

Chapter 19: Taking Stock

Chapter 20: Gossip Girl

## Energetic

Chapter 21: Space Clearing: Home Sweet Home

# Awareness

## +

## Action

## =

# Change

# INTRODUCTION

*Clearing your clutter begins with one step.*

## WHO I AM

I'm an award-winning professional life organizer, author, and certified life coach. I also host the successful self-help podcast *Clear Your Clutter Inside & Out*. I'm the owner of *Reawaken Your Brilliance* and have been in business since July 2009. I have worked with thousands of people through coaching, professional organizing, classes, and presentations.

What motivates me every morning is supporting people in clearing clutter in all areas of their lives, getting organized, and becoming more mindful and aware. When you clear your clutter you can create the life you desire. When you follow your passions, you share your gifts. When you reveal your talents to the world, you not only support others but also give people permission to find their expertise and abilities. This is a world I desire to live in and I strive to make this a reality each day.

## WHY I CREATED THIS BOOK

I view clutter a little bit differently from most professional organizers; most focus solely on the physical clutter. Thankfully, that trend is changing and many professional organizers and other authors are beginning to also include mental clutter as something that should be a part of the clutter-clearing process. For me, clutter goes beyond mental and physical. My definition of clutter is this: *clutter is anything that prevents you from creating the life you choose, deserve, and desire.* I know many of us find ourselves struggling with emotional, spiritual, or energetic clutter as well as having clutter in our relationships, health, and finances.

In my work as a transformational coach and professional life organizer, I witnessed that when people cleared physical clutter, inner clutter was also released. Likewise, when people removed inner clutter they began to release clutter on the outside. When you let go of what no longer serves you, whether physical objects or emotional patterns, you can call into your life what you truly desire.

On September 2, 2014, I first aired my podcast and videos, *Clear Your Clutter Inside & Out,* because I saw there was a need to fill. Just as there was a need for self-help podcasts about clutter, I believe there is a need for books as well. Many books tell you how to remove the physical clutter, but don't touch on other areas. Sometimes you can't simply ask if something brings you joy when deciding whether to keep or discard physical clutter if you have other issues and challenges getting in the way. Being told someone else can get better use of an item might not enable you to let something go. And some people won't want to examine inner clutter and are focused on getting rid of all their physical clutter.

There is no one size fits all when it comes to decluttering, and my hope is that this book will resonate with others who, like me, have sensed that clutter in one part of their lives affects other areas of their lives. If it doesn't work for you, I wish you well on your journey to find what does. It's a win win for all when we each clear our clutter.

The subjects addressed in this book are based on years of working with clients and identifying areas where we all struggle, yet which can serve to build a strong foundation for continued personal growth.

# YOU'VE GOT THIS!

If you purchased this book and have had clutter for a long time, chances are you might be feeling overwhelmed, anxious, or even scared. Know that you are not alone. You may have had friends, family, or even a professional organizer judge your clutter and/or embarrass you. No matter what happened, try and leave those unpleasant experiences in the past and concentrate on the present moment. The present moment is your point of power to change.

Know that you can do this. Even if you've never cleared your clutter or done any self-examination, it's within your abilities. So many times you sell yourself short and underestimate what you can accomplish. Whether it takes you one month, six months, one year or longer, congratulate yourself for taking the first step to forge ahead in releasing clutter from your life.

You can engage with this book alone and keep it private; you don't have to share your answers with anybody. However, it may support you if you share with a trusted friend, coach, therapist, or professional organizer. Choose what feels right for you *right now*. It's okay to change your mind at any time.

Practice deep breathing and take breaks when you need. Honor your pace and don't set yourself up with unrealistic timetables. Pledge to take a step forward in some way every day—no matter how small. If you commit to answering the questions and creating *Take Action* plans, you'll change your life. Little steps add up to big wins.

I encourage you to remember you are "perfect" as an "imperfect" you. Reading this book and taking action is about progress, not perfection. I used to think that there was some final destination I was supposed to reach. I wasn't sure what it looked like, where or what it was, or when I'd reach it, but I believed it was out there. I no longer take that view. Life is about learning, living, loving, and experiencing. It's about growing and becoming more of who you're meant to be.

On the next page is a pledge, and I hope you'll review, sign, and honor it. Be your own best friend, not your own worst enemy. Know that I'm cheering you on because I know you've got this!

When you clear your clutter you can share your gifts with the world. You have important talents and the world needs them now more than ever. Don't let clutter hold you back.

# PLEDGE

I encourage you to customize, or create a similar agreement, and sign below.

I_____, promise myself that I will do my best to be fully present during this process. With purpose and determination, I will read this book and create a plan to clear my clutter. I understand this process might bring up uncomfortable issues and emotions. I will address these feelings to the best of my ability and seek professional support if necessary. I will honor myself to take action to declutter my life with clarity and determination. I will work to create a vision for my home and/or life that I choose, deserve, and desire.

I commit:
- I am dedicated to clearing my inner and outer clutter.
- I am honoring my pace and trusting the process.
- I will not shame, make fun, or be mean to myself.
- I will appreciate all that I am in each moment.
- I will consciously be positive and support myself as I transform my life.
- I will do my best to not buy anything non-essential while I release physical clutter.
- I am focusing on the present.
- I am taking care of myself physically, emotionally, mentally, and spiritually to the best of my ability.
- I am seeking outside support, as I need it.

- I am finding positive ways of handling stress/problems/challenges other than shopping or engaging in other negative behaviors.
- I am prioritizing healing myself, decluttering, and taking action.
- I am acknowledging and honoring myself as I make progress and rewarding myself in healthy ways.
- I am good enough, worthy, and loved, no matter what.

I will also:


Signature:                                    Date:

# HOW TO USE THIS BOOK

The book is divided into four main sections dealing with clutter: physical, mental, emotional, and spiritual. It also includes a bonus chapter on energetic clutter. Within each section, there are five chapters that focus on different subjects. At the end of each chapter, you'll have *Take Action* exercises, which encourage you to move forward.

As you read through the book, you might think to yourself, "I wouldn't call this spiritual clutter; it feels like emotional clutter to me." I encourage you to not spend time and energy on whether the type of clutter was classified "correctly." My hope is that you view the entire book as an umbrella and see that all the subjects fit together in some way. Some chapters may include clutter that could easily be included in another section. For example, in the self-care chapter that is in the emotional clutter section, I mention some thoughts on spirituality and how you can increase taking better care of yourself. To make it easier for you, I kept the theme of a chapter together rather than separate it out into a distinct clutter category.

What's important is that you keep reading, assessing yourself honestly, and taking concrete steps to make real change in your life. In an early draft of this book, a friend pointed out that I repeated a few things. That was deliberate because you may not read every chapter in this book; I wanted to create each chapter as a potential stand-alone so you wouldn't be overwhelmed. Also, many times we need to hear suggestions multiple times, and in different ways and contexts, before we can make a change. Concepts that are really important I mentioned more than once, such as Awareness + Action = Change because so many people aren't able, or willing, to recognize they've overlooked a part of the equation yet still struggle to understand why their life hasn't changed.

No matter what, reading this book and answering these questions will add to your knowledge about yourself. You might discover elements that will help you with your perspective, self-care, and self-kindness. You might even have an epiphany or two along the way. But to truly get the full benefit of this book, I highly encourage you to do the *Take Action* exercises. If you read the book and don't do anything, your life won't change. I want to enable you to change your life; that's why I wrote this book! When you clear your clutter you can share your gifts, and I would love to live in a world where everyone is sharing his or her gifts. Wouldn't you?

You can start at the beginning, where you feel guided, or in any chapter where you think you need the most change. What's most important is that you begin! Don't put yourself on some timetable to get everything done. I suggest reading the book once all the way through and then beginning again with the chapter where you are most compelled to start. I also suggest having a writing tablet, app, computer, or the companion-guided workbook *Clear Your Clutter Inside & Out* to record your *Take Action* exercises. Record your thoughts, feelings, and to-dos as you read the book. Make notes as you read each chapter; that way you have a solid game plan to forge ahead.

My recommendation is to block out time to read the chapters thoughtfully and to create your list of what needs to be done. Do this at a time when you have energy, can easily focus, and don't feel rushed. If you read when you're tired or when you can't concentrate, your mind may go on autopilot and fresh answers might be more challenging to come by.

Sit where it's quiet and you can be uninterrupted. If you're struggling, close your eyes so you can focus. Don't censor yourself; let the answers flow. You can go back through and clarify later. If you're feeling really stuck, refer back to the section on your motivations and what clutter is costing you, as sometimes that can prompt an answer.

Your ego is your image, the mask you wear in front of others, and your titles and roles. On the other hand, your soul is your true essence, authentic self, and is something that is constant and doesn't change. I always recommend going with your intuition/gut instinct/first response when answering a question or creating a list of what steps you need to take. It's my experience that when you say your intuition or gut instinct was "wrong" that you were most likely listening to your ego and not your soul. If you prefer to think through the chapters, consider your typical behavior or how you would respond more often than not. It's most important to be honest so your answers and actions can support you in clearing clutter.

Honor your pace and commit to spending time working through the chapters of the book. Write it down on your project list or make reading a weekend exercise. Ten minutes a day, or 70 minutes on the weekend, accumulates in a year. There's a lot you can accomplish in just over 60 hours! Add *Take Action* exercises to your daily to-do list or make it a weekly or weekend routine.

Please consider getting support when you need it. While some of you can read this book and do it all yourself, others may need help. Remember there's no shame in needing assistance and it's a sign of strength to allow yourself to be vulnerable.

It's important, however, to make sure that you have kind, loving, and helpful support. Remember the old adage, "Don't go to the hardware store for milk." In other words, if your friend or family member is critical, harsh, or judgmental as you work through your clutter, or even worse, makes your experience about them, don't let these people be your group of support. Choose friends and family who only have your best interest at heart. Or find a professional who you trust and feel comfortable working with as you tackle your clutter.

→ Take Action:

- Decide how you choose to use this book.
- Have a writing tablet, app, smart phone/computer, or *Clear Your Clutter Inside & Out* companion guide, to record thoughts as you read.
- Fill out and sign the pledge.
- Consider reading the entire book once and then starting where you feel most guided.
- Begin reading and Take Action!

# TAKE ACTION

When you write things down, you're more likely to complete your tasks.

You can read all the books in the library, listen to world-renowned healers, follow all the gurus on social media, and participate in numerous retreats, but if you don't do the work, your life will never change.

I encourage you to create a strategy to clear clutter from your life. When you are reviewing your answers, what resonates with you? Is there a question that sparks a realization or motivates you to remove clutter right away? What can you reasonably accomplish in a daily or weekly practice? What's feasible given your lifestyle and commitments? What other questions can you contemplate? These are just a few of the considerations that can support you in formulating strategies to clear your clutter.

You can start to release clutter immediately or you can wait until you've read the book cover to cover. You may decide to use this book as a companion guide to support you as you begin clearing clutter. Do what works for you and honor your pace, but I encourage you to *do something*!

Once you've completed a section, or the book, take time to develop your *Take Action* strategy. Without taking steps to move forward, your discoveries and moments of clarity won't make much difference.

Here are a few strategies when creating steps to clear your clutter:

*Make SMART (specific, measurable, achievable, relevant, and time-bound) goals.* The more specific and realistic your goal, the more likely you'll achieve it (e.g. *I choose to lose 15 pounds in four months; I'll spend 20 minutes each day decluttering my office over the next week*).

*Keep it real.* Rome wasn't built in a day, but you can probably declutter your closet in one. Tackle no more than one or two items because some habits are challenging to change. Set a date to check your progress.

*Show yourself compassion.* If you're trying to lose weight because of the emotional clutter from having an argument with a friend, and eat a bag of chocolate, don't beat yourself up. Get back on the horse and recommit to moving forward.

*Be accountable.* How can you track your progress? Can you share what you're doing with a trusted friend? Use an app? When you're challenged, remind yourself what you're gaining from achieving your goals as well as what you're no longer losing. How else will you remain motivated?

*Find support.* Seek ways to gain help and wisdom from others. You can seek feedback from someone who has accomplished the same goal, work with a friend, or join a group with similar goals. If you remain stuck, consider professional guidance.

*Go with the flow.* Life happens; small steps count. If losing 15 pounds is too much, can you start with five? You can always amend your goals.

*Stay the course.* Whether you make changes right away or it takes a year, remaining positive and keeping focused on your goal is an accomplishment.

*Celebrate your progress.* Practice enjoying your personal growth and development, and reward yourself in healthy ways.

Many times people who have a lot of clutter are also challenged when it comes to making decisions, and arriving at decisions often means making choices. The good news is that you can learn how to make choices. My nickname in college was "Indecisive One," yet the steps I've taken to declutter my life have allowed me to more easily make decisions. If I can learn how to, you can too! Here are some tips for decision-making:

- Go with your gut response or intuition. It's there to guide you.
- Set standards: "I'll make a decision once I know A, B, and C." Once you have answers, make a choice.
- Consult a friend who has been through the same issue.
- Ask yourself if the decision is really meaningful. Will it matter a day, week, month, or year from now? If not, make a judgment or flip a coin.
- Make a list of the pros and cons. Prioritize which considerations are most important to you.
- Set a deadline to research facts and information to assess your options.
- Brainstorm and come up with several choices. Determine if the options are compatible with

your values, interests, and abilities.

- Re-read your priorities to help guide you to making a choice.
- Weigh possible outcomes. What's the worst that can happen? What will happen if you do A, B, or C? Can you live with the consequences?
- Establish a **deadline** to make a final decision.

I also encourage you to create an *Immediate Take Action* plan. You may have several items of clutter that you need to address. Review your *Take Action* list and pick no more than three items to complete *right now*. Focus on a few of your changes to implement, and before you know it you'll have made real progress.

I'm relying on you to govern yourself according to your circumstances. If you need more guidance in dealing with what you discover, are challenged, or feeling paralyzed and stuck, consider hiring a coach, therapist, or professional organizer. You can also ask a trusted, non-judgmental friend or family member for support.

Let me say this again: consider hiring a coach, therapist, or professional organizer. My editor pointed out to me in an early draft that many of my Take Action's included "seek professional support if necessary." I wasn't aware I was repeating myself in almost every chapter. Apologies if I still mention this a little too much for your liking. Obviously, it's a point I feel very strongly about emphasizing. In fact, it may be the most important suggestion I share. There's no shame in asking or receiving professional support. If you need to, I really, really, really, hope you'll do so.

Our first section focuses on physical clutter, followed by mental, emotional, and spiritual. I'll provide examples throughout the chapters so you can see how clutter may be showing up in your life. At the end of each chapter, you'll find your *Take Action's* with step-by-step guidance. Finally, after the bonus Chapter 21, is the *Immediate Take Action* plan, with instructions, which is optional.

# WHY AM I MOTIVATED TO CLEAR CLUTTER?

Why did you buy this book? Are your finances in shambles because you don't pay your bills on time? Does your mind never seem to shut down? Are you overwhelmed by your emotions? Do you spend your energy comparing yourself to others?

Take the time to really answer why you're motivated to clear clutter. Building a strong foundation for motivation will support you when you become challenged. One of my strongest motivations in clearing the physical clutter in my office was to build my business and increase my creativity. Your motivation might be to learn a new language, travel the world, set up an animal sanctuary, get out of debt, make peace with your past, have a better retirement, change jobs, heal yourself, start a new hobby, go back to school, develop a business idea, mend a broken relationship, downsize, etc.

Record your motivations to release clutter and how the clutter makes you feel. Also, document how your life will improve when you release the clutter.

Review your motivations when you're struggling to answer a question or feeling overwhelmed in doing your *Take Action* strategy.

**EXAMPLES:**

## Physical

*My physical clutter is everywhere! It makes me feel like a bad wife and bad mom. Why can't I keep a tidy house? I feel sad and overwhelmed when I look at my space. I'm hoping when I release my junk, I can easily find my keys when I need them and my mother-in-law will stop her snippy comments about how her home is always tidy and mine isn't. I want to quit feeling guilt about all this stuff.*

## Mental

*Where do I begin with my mental clutter? It's worry about the future that keeps me up at night. This mind chatter makes me feel overwhelmed, hopeless, and stressed out. I feel like I never get a moment just to relax and be present. I'd like my life to improve with better sleep and less worry. I'd like to be hopeful when I think about the future and focus on all the possibilities instead of being scared.*

## Emotional

*Boy am I grateful no one can read this, as I'm really embarrassed to write this. I have sooooo much anger inside. It's like every little thing ticks me off! You'd think someone cutting me off in traffic was the end of the world. All this anger exhausts me. It's also isolated me a bit as some of my friends no longer want to hang out. I'd like to feel in control of my emotions. I want to get to the root of the anger so I can release it. I'd like to have more meaningful relationships.*

## Spiritual

*At first I really wasn't sure what to write about spiritual clutter. Then I thought about it and realized I gossip a lot. I hadn't really noticed it until someone called me out at work asking, "Is there any celebrity you don't gossip about?" When I gossip, I feel good at first but then I feel bad later. It's like eating a decadent dessert and feeling the effects later. I don't feel better about myself. I feel sad I waste time judging others. I'd like to spend my time improving my life. I'd like to see the good in everyone and not their flaws. I'd like to unburden my judgment.*

## Your Motivation

Now it's your turn to figure out what problem you'd like to solve by releasing clutter. The more details you have the more motivation you'll have to release your clutter. Feel free to come back and add to this list at any time.

What's my physical clutter?

How does my physical clutter make me feel?

How do I hope will my life improve once I release my physical clutter?

What's my mental clutter?

How does my mental clutter make me feel?

How do I hope my life improve once I let go of my mental clutter?

What's my emotional clutter?

How does my emotional clutter make me feel?

How do I hope my life improve once I free my emotional clutter?

What's my spiritual clutter?

How does my spiritual clutter make me feel?

How do I hope my life improves once I emancipate my spiritual clutter?

# WHAT'S CLUTTER COSTING ME?

Have you really, truly thought about what clutter costs you? Do you fight with your spouse or partner over all that you own? Have you experienced insomnia because you're anxious about the future? Do you find yourself in an unfulfilling job? Are you suppressing your true feelings through an unhealthy habit such as overeating?

Clutter costs you peace of mind, increases stress, reduces the quality of your relationships, negatively impacts your health, costs you time and money, and much more. By writing down the true cost of your clutter, you can use what you're losing to inspire and power through, especially when you feel stuck. Be as specific as you're able to when recording your thoughts.

Record what clutter is costing you and how it makes you feel. Also, document what you'll gain when you release your clutter. Take the time to honestly answer these questions. Really understanding what clutter is truly costing you will help you overcome your reluctance and resistance you may have to releasing it.

Examine what you're losing when you're grappling to create a strategy or feeling overwhelmed in taking action.

## EXAMPLES:

### Physical
*I gathered all my electronics that were collecting dust in the house. Dang! I never realized how much junk we had we weren't using. I did some Googling and found I can sell most of this stuff for about a thousand bucks. I had no clue how*

*much money I was losing and I feel stupid. We'll get a nice vacation this year after I sell all the items.*

## Mental
*Clutter is costing me peace of mind because my husband and I fight over clutter almost daily. He keeps claiming he doesn't see it and I just want to scream, "It's everywhere!" I'm tired of trying to stay on top of it all and getting him to care about how it drives me crazy. I want to fight less and spend time enjoying each other's company and having fun—that's what I hope I'll gain.*

## Emotional
*I keep stuffing my mouth with food because I am so stressed and overwhelmed with all this clutter. Instead of expressing how angry I am that my roommate has all her stuff all over the apartment, I eat instead. I never made the connection until now that her clutter was costing me my health. I hope to have better health and lose the stress and not fight with my roommate.*

## Spiritual
*I'm sick and tired of everyone in my family complaining all the time about what they don't have! We have so much compared to so many people. I spend thousands on gifts for the family throughout the year. As I'm writing this, I have to admit the kids get their lack of gratitude from me. I always manage to find the worst in everything. This makes me feel sad, angry, and exhausted. I'd like for us to be closer as a family and not spend so much time on the physical stuff. I'd like to gain a sense of gratitude for all I have and focus on the positive more.*

## Your Losses

Now it's your turn to figure out what clutter is costing you. The more details you have the more motivation you'll have to release your clutter. What comes to you immediately? Feel free to come back and add to this list at any time.

My clutter is costing me:

1.

2.

3.

4.

5.

6.

7.

8.

9.

10.

What I'm losing because of clutter makes me feel:

1.

2.

3.

4.

5.

6.

7.

8.

9.

10.

What I hope to gain when I release my clutter:

1.

2.

3.

4.

5.

6.

7.

8.

9.

10.

# PHYSICAL

People have different levels of comfort with the number of possessions they own. To a minimalist, my house is cluttered. I love paintings from where I've travelled; I have a set of dishes for entertaining, and a full bookcase that brings me joy. However, I can find what I need when I need it, don't have stuff everywhere, and I can relax in my home. I also use everything I own and release clutter annually. To the minimalist, I'd respond that although I have a lot of objects in my home, they all have a use.

It's been my experience the more you clear physical clutter, the easier the clearing becomes. Remember, this is a process. If you're not ready to part with anything, that's absolutely fine and I recommend never forcing yourself to do so. Don't get rid of anything if doing so increases your stress. Be gentle with yourself; you're taking action.

When you clear your physical clutter you can focus on what's important to you and create room to devote time to what really matters. As you clear your physical areas, pay attention to how you feel. For example, do you find more mental clarity? Are you less stressed emotionally as you aren't dealing with so much stuff? Does what you truly desire become more apparent as you let go of what you don't want?

# Trust you will get what you need when you need it.

# Chapter 1

## Let's Get Physical

*If everything has the same value then nothing is valuable.*

What I mean by the above quote is that if you're challenged to let go of items because you see everything as valuable, then you'll never be able to release anything. If a diamond necklace has the same value as costume jewelry, or an antique chair has the same value as a chair from Ikea, value serves as an excuse to keep everything. Exercising discernment and understanding what's important can go a long way in releasing clutter.

*The clutter in her home overwhelmed Jeri. She was angry with herself because she wasn't able to easily declutter her possessions. Jeri shared, "I'm smart, accomplished at work, and a task master. Why can't I do this?" Her frustration was palpable. I explained to her that many times the clutter is the outward manifestation of something else and sometimes it takes a neutral, non-judgmental person to help you gain a new perspective.*

*I immediately noticed a huge stack of paper about three feet tall. I asked Jeri what the pile was. She told me they were clippings that she was going to send to people. Jeri explained she cut interesting articles from newspapers and magazines that she thought friends and family would enjoy. She spent a ton of time not only cutting and mailing but also in searching to find informative pieces for many people every month. Sending notes to many people took up precious time that she couldn't devote to her beloved music. I asked her how long she had had these pieces. She shyly responded, "A few years."*

*As we dug a little deeper, Jeri shared it stressed her to always be searching, trimming, and stuffing. "I feel like this is all I do in my free time. And when I finally decide to take a moment for myself, the pile shames and judges me. I don't know how to get ahead of it all." I probed some more and suddenly Jeri had a light bulb moment. She exclaimed, "I'm afraid if I don't keep in touch with my loved ones and let them know I'm thinking about them that they won't love me anymore!" As soon as she voiced this, Jeri knew that it wasn't true. Whether or not Jeri sent them clippings had no affect on how people cared for her.*

*We promptly sent all of the papers into the recycling bin!*

Sometimes with physical clutter, there is something much deeper happening. Like Jeri did, see if you could reflect on why you may be holding on to certain objects. If you're able to get to the root of the problem, it's easier to let things go and regularly release what no longer serves you.

This chapter outlines the process I use when working with a customer. My goal is for my clients, and you, to think through the process of decluttering. Hopefully, in this process, you'll have some a-ha moments. My desire is that the other chapters under physical clutter will support you even more. If you're buying a book that's talking about releasing physical clutter, I feel it should include some basics. Before I ever became a professional organizer, I read Julie Morgenstern's *Organizing from the Inside Out*. It's arguably the best book on organizing. I learned the basics from her book and have refined and incorporated my own techniques.

## Getting Started

"A stitch in time saves nine", as the saying goes. It's worth it for you to take time at the beginning to **devise a blueprint to move forward**. I encourage my clients to go through <u>everything</u> they own annually. Once you've done a thorough purge of your space, it's much easier to maintain. If you haven't gone through your clutter in 20 years you'll most likely have more stuff than you did after a year.

Start by taking an inventory of your home, office, or space. As you look at each room or area, consider what needs an overhaul, what needs some tweaking, and what's fine as is. When I do my annual purge, I literally write down on a piece of paper a list of all my rooms. I then break down each room into smaller items. My office includes:

- Julie bookcase.
- Tony bookcase.
- Large desk.
- Filing cabinet.
- Small desk.

You can also break down each area further. For example, my large desk would be: computer, desk surface, left drawer, and right drawer.

After you've done that, take the time to **prioritize your list**. Many times my customers are so overwhelmed that they have no idea where they should begin, even after creating their list. I encourage them to ask questions such as:

- Impending deadline? Something may not be urgent, but you still have a deadline. You're getting cabinets installed in the garage and it needs to be cleaned out by a certain date.
- What areas are absolutely driving you crazy? Are you going nuts because you can't sleep on your bed because it's covered in clothes?
- Anything urgent? If your office is a mess and you can't find your bills and you're losing money, start in your office.
- Where do you spend most of your time? If your family enjoys hanging out in the TV room, begin clearing that clutter so you can get back to family time.

If you're really overwhelmed, I suggest picking a small project to ease into the decluttering process. Shelves on a bookcase, a drawer in your kitchen, or cleaning out your wallet or purse are projects that can usually be done easily and quickly and help build your confidence.

Once you figure out where you'll begin, take the time to **schedule your project**. Would you like to try and complete it over a weekend? Could it be done after work for an hour each evening? Do you want to try and devote two hours a week? Be realistic about your time. However long you think it will take, double that time. Very rarely have I seen a project take less time than what was planned.

Next, **commit to decluttering by blocking off time** on your calendar. If you don't write what you need to do down, your to-dos tend not to get "to-done". Focus on completing one room, area, or project at a time. Don't move onto another project until you complete the one you started. Do you want some good news? I have found, as have my clients, that the more you declutter, the easier it becomes.

Finally, let's have some fun. Decluttering can be challenging, boring for some, and take some physical effort. **Create a vision for each room** and what you want to feel when you spend time in each area or space. In my office I desire a space where I'm creative, tackle my daily tasks, and make an income to support my cats in the lifestyle they've become accustomed to enjoying. When I walk into my office I need to feel inspired, energized, focused, and joyful.

I always have my clients write their vision and what they **would like to experience and feel in each space.** If you want to go all out, create a vision board. At the very least, have a written list of how you want your space to look, feel like, and what activities you'll do in your newly decluttered space. Your vision can serve as a great motivator when you're trudging through and want to quit!

Don't forget to wear clothes that you can throw in the laundry later and sturdy shoes as you may be doing a bit of walking, lifting, dusting, and moving all day. Before you begin to declutter, gather your supplies. Here are my suggestions:

- *Music.* Calming, zydeco, techno--whatever you need to keep you motivated and going strong.
- *Beverages and snacks.* Make sure you keep hydrated and well fed. Going to get a snack or a drink can be an excuse to stop decluttering. Set yourself up for success.
- *Writing pad, pen or pencil, or an app.* Questions and concerns may come up such as "Ask accountant if I can release 2015 tax returns", or "Ask Aunt Mary about grandmother's bookcase." Don't try to remember, jot down questions, thoughts, and concerns.
- *Boxes and/or trash bags.* Make sure they aren't going to easily fall apart. The last thing you want to have happen is be walking down the stairs and have a bag burst. Don't make anything super heavy as you could hurt yourself. Bend from your knees when lifting!
- *Paper or index cards & tape to label piles.* (I don't recommend post it or sticky notes as I've seen too many move or fly away.) I suggest the following categories: *Keep, Donate, Return, Repair, Recycle, Sell, Give to Friends/Family, Another Location, and Trash*. Another category may come up, so have something on hand to label. You may think you'll remember, but as you begin to declutter you may get your piles confused or you may use forgetting as an excuse to keep stuff.
- *Vacuum, dust cloth, cleaners, broom, dustpan, spritzer bottle & cloth, and/or air freshener.* While you're decluttering, save some time and do a little cleaning, especially if the area or space is dirty or dusty. I like to use essential oils

in a spritzer bottle with water to freshen a space after I have decluttered.

- *Folders, labels, and pen.* If you're going through files this will help you easily organize items into categories.
- *File box or container for papers.* If you have a lot of paperwork a box or container can keep you more organized as you declutter.

Now that you have your supplies, you're ready to begin. In your room or space, pick a place to get started. In your office, it may be a bookcase. In your kitchen, it might be the pantry. In your bedroom, your closet may be the starting point. You get the idea.

## Step-by-Step Decluttering

I always suggest pulling everything out into the area so you can really take in and see all that you own. So, if you're decluttering jeans, pull them all out and put them on the bed. (Try to avoid the floor as that may mean extra laundry.) Make sure you've done a full sweep of the house so you get all of your jeans, not just what's in your closet or dresser.

If your space is really jam packed, then you might need to **clear some space** to have an area to work. I have found that for most people, finding space is rarely an issue unless you are a hoarder. (A hoarder is someone who has so many possessions that he or she may literally just have a narrow path in a room and might not have a clear space to work.)

It's a good idea to **start with what you can actually see.** If you're in the bedroom, don't start under the bed.

Start with bookshelves, the top of a nightstand, a basket of books, your underwear drawer, etc.

As you're pulling items out, **categorize** the items. It's important that when you categorize, they make sense to you! Mistakes I often see people make are that they read a magazine, their friend is awesome at organizing, or the latest fad says to do it one way and that's the only way it can be done. Decluttering and organizing is individual and one size does not fit all. I alphabetize my phone by first name. Most people do it by last name. For whatever reason, first name works better for me. I do what makes sense to me and I encourage you to do the same.

**Keep your groupings broad and somewhat loose for flexibility.** Don't make them so strict that it will be hard to remember several categories down the road. Even with a file index, you'll most likely tire of keeping up a mega-defined system. As an example, I keep all my socks together without any dividers. I don't differentiate between everyday, exercise, hike, no show, etc. I'd rather spend a few seconds picking out socks than keeping everything super tidy in compartments. If you have a bunch of socks or like to be strictly organized, you may need to do a little more categorizing, but see if a general category can work.

Remember to **focus on one area at a time.** Do one shelf in the bookcase and don't move to the second one until the first is complete. Don't do a little work in your closet and then decide that you need to declutter underneath your bed. If you begin to do this, stop and take a deep breath. Are you trying to avoid something by not completing an area? If that's the case, give yourself a break and come back to it when you're in a frame of mind to deal with something directly.

Once you've categorized now comes the fun part. **Editing!** Most people feel a great sense of relief after they've done some eliminating. I always feel like I've lost 10 pounds.

As you release elements, **put items in one of your labeled boxes, bags, or containers <u>right away</u>.** Packing up items not only saves you time but also encourages you to get your boxes and bags out of the house immediately after you've filled them up.

Letting go of what you own can be challenging, so **go easy on yourself.** Sometimes you may hold on to your possessions for a variety of reasons, such as obligation. You don't like that wedding gift, but are afraid that you'll offend someone if you let it go. How likely is it that people will ask about a wedding gift? If they do ask and get upset at you for letting something go, remember that's their issue and has nothing to do with you. When I give a gift, I give it with no expectations. I tell the recipient I did the best I could, but if I missed the mark, do with it what they please. They can return, sell, donate, or whatever they see fit.

**If you're struggling, here are some questions to get you started.** What other questions can you ask yourself?

- Do I need?
- Do I like?
- Do I love?

- Do I use?
- Does this object make me feel good or bad?
- Does this item bring me fulfillment or joy?
- Is this a need or a want?
- When was the last time I used this thing?
- Is there a family or friend who can use this more?
- Is this object making or costing me money?
- Does it represent who I am now or whom I choose to be?
- Can someone else get better use?
- Why am I resisting releasing this?
- If I had to purchase it again, would I get the exact same thing?
- Is there an online source?
- Who else can benefit from this?

This might sound corny, but I also suggest **thanking the items or objects you are letting go**, especially if you're struggling. Thank the sweater for keeping you warm, the ice skates for bringing you hours of fun, or the book that gave you knowledge. Having a moment of gratitude for all the items have given you can support you in releasing. Everything is energy, so saying thanks really does impact the process.

"Duh!" I hear this from my niece a lot these days. Maybe I'm Captain Obvious when stating a fact or asking a question or maybe it's just how a teenager responds. Using the above questions, some of what you own will be easy to let go. If you **establish some guidelines at the beginning, letting go should be easier**. If you say, "Anything with an expired date goes," then you won't waste time deciding when you're in the middle of decluttering. Trust me, you don't want anything to slow down the process. You can get lost in the land of indecisiveness! It can also be helpful if you're working with trusted family or friends. They know the guidelines and you won't waste time debating.

Here are some of my "DUH! These Go *Right Now*."

- Stuff that has no value to you.
- Pieces you never used, wore, watched, etc.
- Expired: spices, food, make-up, samples, etc.
- Clothes, shoes, and accessories that are too small/too big/uncomfortable/ripped/stained/stretched out/pilled/threadbare, or you don't feel good or great wearing.
- Old and archaic electronics and information, such as dated magazines.
- Non-working tools, devices, appliances, exercise equipment, hairdryers, etc.
- Junk that can't be repaired (broken, rusty, missing parts, etc.).
- Too much of anything.
- Objects you don't like or love.
- Photographs (including digital!) where you hate how you look, they're a bad memory, or are duplicates.
- Borrowed or need to return items.
- Things just gathering dust.
- Items you never really liked or loved and are holding onto for someone else.
- Anything that makes you feel bad or brings up negative or unpleasant feelings, memories, or people no longer in your life.[1]

What else can you add to this list? Don't forget to check out my resource section on my webpage for eco-friendly suggestions to keep clutter out of the landfill!

★*TIP*: *If you wouldn't give it to family members or friends because it's in poor condition, don't dump it on a charity. They probably can't use it either and you just made more work for them. In some states the non-profit may have to pay landfill fees.*

Once you've edited your belongings, **immediately take care of all your piles**. Put the "keep" pieces back where they belong and take the pieces that belong in another location to the right room. Remove the trash and recycling to containers outside. Make a deadline that within two weeks that you'll return or sell because the last thing you want is for all your hard work to morph back into clutter. Take what you're going to donate to the non-profit, find a place outside until you can drop off, or schedule a pick up with a charity. If you're able, put items that need to be returned (store, friend, library, etc.) in your car, so you can take care of those tasks within a few days. If you're overwhelmed, ask your friends to pick up what you'll be giving them, or to make a run to the recycling center or charity.

Finally, don't forget to schedule some time after you've purged. Decluttering can be messy, exhausting, emotionally draining, and sometimes painful. It can also be exhilarating, liberating, and rejuvenating, but I always encourage my customers to **follow a day of decluttering with rest, pampering, humor, and reflection.**

## Suggestions for Children

I'm a firm believer in teaching kids how to declutter and get organized. I've worked with children, including my nieces and nephew, in both of these areas. **Teaching kids at a young age how to declutter and get organized really sets them up for success in life.** I've worked with many people who struggle as adults, and I believe if they had learned these skills as children they wouldn't be saddled with clutter as adults.

- *Establish limits.* The average child in the UK has over 300 toys yet plays with only 12². Check in with yourself, especially if your kids are young, to see if you may be buying more for yourself than for them because of what you experienced as a child. Boundaries make children feel more secure so limit the amount of toys, clothes, games, etc. you purchase and keep in your home.
- *Create routines.* Institute rules for picking up and taking care of belongings. I can't tell you how many parents I see who constantly pick up after their children and then wonder why, as teenagers, their rooms are a disaster or it looks like a hurricane passed through. When we take care of our possessions, they last longer. It teaches children the value of buying something. A dear friend of mine grew up very poor and she takes very good care of everything she owns because if she didn't, she'd go without.
- *Utilize birthdays and holidays.* These occasions are a good time for children (and all of us!) to edit our possessions. As gifts are coming in, make space for the new and release the old.

Getting into a habit helps kids release their possessions more easily.

- *Pick a charity.* If your child sees that something he or she owned is going to a good home, and will help other kids, or a cause he or she cares about, your child has another reason to free what he or she no longer uses and this can aid in letting go.
- *Involve children in decision-making.* When you create memory boxes, do a general purge, or decide what art, paper, and projects to keep from the school year, check in with your children. You may be holding on to something that doesn't mean anything to them, or accidentally throw out something important. Being involved in the decluttering process helps children learn and determine what has worth. If everything has the same value, then nothing is valuable. The toy from the McDonald's is as valuable as the Steiff teddy bear.

Summary
Do all the steps thoroughly and involve each member of your household. Make it a fun effort and reward yourself with good self-care when your tasks have been completed.

➔ Take Actions:

- Do an inventory of your space: needs decluttering; a little bit of clutter clearing; or no work needed.
- Create a vision for each area or room.
- Decide which room or area to begin as well as a list, in order of importance, for other spaces.
- Block out time on your calendar.
- Make a list of supplies you need.

- Gather your supplies.
- Label boxes or garbage bags.
- Determine what questions to ask when eliminating items.
- Begin clearing clutter in one room/area.
- Categorize items in a way that makes sense to you.
- Edit all your piles and release items you no longer use, love, etc.
- Release your Duh's.
- Donate, trash, give to a friend, and/or recycle as soon as possible.
- Make deadlines for what you're going to sell, repair, give to a friend, or return to owner.
- Support your kids in clearing clutter.
- Schedule self-care post decluttering.

# Chapter 2

## What's Your Kryptonite?

*What you collect reflects what you feel is missing from your life.*

Are you someone who always purchases the 10 for 10 deals at Kroger even if you never eat them? How many collections do you own? What is it that you cannot resist buying more of no matter what? What makes you go crazy and believe that you must buy <u>right now</u>?

What's your clutter kryptonite?

Like Superman, you become weak and fall to your knees. It's as if aliens control your mind and you must *buy now*. You're compelled to purchase things, even if you know you already have the exact same item at home. Or you're on autopilot and buy something similar because you just have to have it! Perhaps you're convinced that a product is the answer to all your problems.

You think because I'm a professional organizer and declutter for a living that I don't have clutter kryptonite? Of course I do! Here's what overwhelms and embarrasses me, and where I can easily lose all my clutter busting skills. The first is make-up samples. If you tell me a product will reduce my wrinkles, or give me flawless skin, I can't take the free trials out of the clerk's hands fast enough. The problem is that I end up with a drawer full of personal care products that have expired. And I would clean it out every year frustrated I'd never used the samples. I hate throwing anything out and would get upset with myself that once again, despite the best intentions, I was foiled by my clutter kryptonite.

The other area where I'm challenged is leopard print. I could probably wear leopard print most days and be happy. I love love love leopard print! Luckily, I know what looks good on me and what styles, shapes, and prints to avoid. However, I could go crazy and buy a lot more. Leopard print for every day of the week anyone? I have to watch myself, especially with shoes. It would be really easy for me to pick up another pair of leopard print boots or footwear.

You aren't alone when it comes to having clutter kryptonite.

*Pam collected stuffed animals. Her bedroom, guest room, and living room had creatures of all sizes and shapes. Pam was struggling to pare down her collection because they were affecting her relationships. Friends and family were judgmental about the furry creatures that overwhelmed her space. The judgments of others made Pam withdraw from people even more.*

*When we were working together, I asked Pam when she first started collecting her stuffed animals. She shared that she had always had them as a child. Instead of imaginary friends, Pam had her furry ones to talk to. She shared that her collection exploded after she moved to Seattle after college. None of her college friends were close and she had a hard time making friends. On more than one occasion, Pam's "friends" mistreated her. As we were sorting all of her stuffed animals, she made the connection that she was substituting her stuffed animals for real friendships. Pam was afraid to let them go because they never hurt her. These stuffed creatures represented connection and friendship for Pam. We talked more about how she had put up a wall that was not only affecting her friendships but also potential romantic partners.*

*After understanding why she was still collecting, she was able to weed through her stuffed animals, and stop buying them. Pam worked on being able to recognize when people were trying to take advantage of her, how to let her guard down with friends who truly cared about her, and she was able to strengthen her connection to her family.*

The key, and what I teach my clients, is to **know what your clutter kryptonite is and then stay aware** so your home doesn't become overrun, and you don't become frustrated and overwhelmed. If I can learn to do it and put a plan in place, you can as well. Decluttering is not a superpower; it's simply staying on top of areas where you're challenged.

As I mentioned earlier, **Awareness + Action = Change.**

If Superman encounters kryptonite, he can't use his superpowers to save the world. Similarly, if you live in clutter you can't focus on what's important and share your gifts.

First step: become aware of your clutter kryptonite. Look around your home. What do you seem to have a lot of or collect? Take the time to contemplate if necessary. What is it that you buy all the time, sale or not? If you're stumped, ask your friends or family. Who knows you well and can give you honest feedback? Where do they see you go weak in the knees and buy, buy, buy? It may be subtle, like my make up-samples, or more obvious like leopard print clothes and shoes. You may need to spend some time becoming aware. Don't put a timeline on yourself. **Start by observing and paying attention to what you buy** and notice how many you already have of something. Where, and when, do you seem to be on autopilot when it comes to buying?

★*TIP: Take the time to count the number of your clutter kryptonite items. Do you collect shot glasses, pennants, figurines, electronics, etc.? You may be surprised at how many "unknown" collections you have. For extra credit, count how many things you own in each collection. Can you pare down?*

What's important is to not judge yourself and go down that rabbit hole. Judging yourself wastes time and energy and keeps you from the important work of decluttering.

Instead, **be like an archeologist or scientist searching for information.** When you spin your wheels and get caught up in judgment, you're less likely to move forward and actually take action because you're focusing on judging yourself. Beating yourself up isn't going to change anything and you can waste precious time getting sidetracked by admonishing yourself.

You're not alone; we all have challenges. If you're surrounded by clutter, there's a good chance you're already hard on yourself for having clutter. Be your own best friend here, not your worst enemy. You're taking steps to clear your clutter and that is important. Focus on the progress you're making.

It's worth **spending the time to figure out** <u>why</u> **you're collecting.** Right after I was a victim of a crime while living in Los Angeles, I started collecting angels. To me angels represent love and protection, something I felt I didn't have. It wasn't until a decade later when I read a book on Feng Shui that I made the connection. Once I had that a-ha moment, I no longer felt the need to collect angels. (I still have many angels because they make me happy and I feel they watch over our space, but I rarely buy any more.)

Despite my frustration for taking so long to figure this out, I was gentle with myself. How could I be angry with myself for trying to find comfort? I began to look for other ways I could make myself feel loved and protected.

What's your clutter kryptonite saying to you? **What need are you trying to fulfill?** It doesn't have to be from a traumatic experience. For instance, I figured out one of the reasons I collected make-up samples was because I didn't feel attractive. I worked on my self-esteem, being authentic, and putting the best version of me forward, and now I pick up samples only when I <u>really</u> want to try a specific product. It's worth the time to figure this out because most often, once you do, your need to collect disappears.

When you figure out your need, **what other healthier experiences/thoughts/activities can you use to meet that desire?** If you buy something to feel loved, how can you find love? Perhaps you schedule a massage, say affirmations, or ask close friends what they admire about you.

Once you've pinpointed where you're challenged, have a strategy to make sure you don't buy your clutter kryptonite. Here are some suggestions:

- Have a list when you go into the store and stick to it!
- Pick an accountability buddy you can call or text when you're feeling weak.
- Set a monetary amount you won't go over, have a credit card limit, or only use cash.
- Let friends and family know you're working on decluttering and ask that they don't buy you gifts for your collection. Suggest alternatives, such as experiences – a cooking class, an afternoon of ice-skating, or theater tickets, or something practical that you use and buy regularly, such as cleaning supplies.
- Figure out a healthy habit to do when the urge for your clutter kryptonite appears. I take a deep breath when looking at leopard print. I'll touch it and say, "Isn't that groovy?" and walk away.
- Work with a life coach or therapist if you're really challenged. An outside, non-judgmental voice can support you in getting to the root of why you collect and help you make a plan to change your spending habits.

Summary
Your clutter kryptonite is the physical stuff that you can't say no to and collect no matter how much you own.

## ➜ Take Actions:

- Write down the different items you own a lot of, or collect.
- Ask a trusted friend or family member if you're unsure of your clutter kryptonite.
- Gather all items from one collection and purge three things immediately.
- Continue to comb through your clutter kryptonite.
- Remove all your purged possessions from your house.
- Figure out what deeper need you're trying to fill.
- Find healthy alternatives to fill that desire.
- Stop buying your clutter kryptonite.

# Chapter 3

## Memories Light the Corners of My Mind

*Memories aren't in objects; they are in your heart and head.*

Objects that hold memories can be one of the most difficult possessions to let go. Remember, **if everything has the same value then nothing is valuable.**

It can also be really challenging when you're given pieces that have been in the family for years, if not generations. I can't tell you how many people I know who have family "heirlooms" boxed up that they haven't looked at in 20+ years that are just collecting dust. My clients will say, "But it was my mom's", or "My favorite great aunt gave it to me."

*I was very close with my paternal grandmother and feel very fortunate to have had her as a guiding light in my life. I still feel her presence, wisdom, and love even now that's she passed to the next adventure.*

*After my grandmother died, my father and my aunts were very generous about dividing her possessions to all the family members. I was living in California at the time and they shipped me everything, including her childhood bedroom set. The set is over 100 years old and was the furniture in my aunts' room growing up. It's now in our guest bedroom. I cherish it for many reasons: it's antique, it's the bed I slept in when I would visit my grandmother, and it reminds me of her every day. Plus, it's useful for visitors.*

*They also sent me a set of my grandmother's dishes. If memory serves, these were dishes that sat in the basement of her home for years. I'm betting she got them for free when she opened up a bank account. At one time, they were white with yellow and green daisies surrounding the rim. The dishes were no longer white when I received them; they were grayish and the now dingy flowers colors had worn.*

*Even though they were ugly and I wouldn't use them, I didn't want to let them go because they were my grandmother's. At the time, I believed that they represented her and kept her in my life. If I donated the dishes, I'd be letting go of my grandmother. Would I be disrespecting her or not honoring what she meant to me? Would she be upset, watching my every move from the other side? And my biggest fear: would she stop loving me or would my memories of her fade?*

*A few months later, I saw Peter Walsh [3] speak at a meeting for a group I volunteered with on clearing clutter.*

*Peter talked about our memories being in our heads and not in the contents of our material goods. That was a big a-ha moment for me. I donated my grandmother's dishes the next day. I kept the important and useful furnishings (like the bedroom set) that I cherished. I let the other junk go. Many times my customers have those insights when they figure out why they are holding on to a particular piece. Once you know you're releasing an object and not the person or the experience, you usually are able to let go of what you might have held onto for years.*

As I have continued to work with clients, and have done my own personal wellness work, I believe that your memories are not only in your head, but also in your heart. When you let go of the object, you still have the memories and the love. The recollections won't leave you when the object does.

## Working with Memories

What I tell my customers, and what I truly believe, is that when people pass on they want you to be happy and free and they give you permission to let go. And if this doesn't ring true for you, the reality is they aren't here to fight you. Seriously, you aren't doing them any harm by releasing what you don't love, like, use, or need.

It can be a **process to relinquish all the furnishings that have memories** (good and bad) associated with them. I was in an on/off relationship for a really long time. It took me almost two years to release everything. When I knew it was finally over, and I had closure, I was able to recycle, shred, donate, and trash it all. They key was, I stuck with it and every six months or so, I would go through the lone box every few months until it was empty.

★*TIP: Have a conversation with the possessions you are releasing. Sometimes acknowledging how an item has served you can support you in letting it go. Thank the sweater for the memories of good times, express gratitude for the boots that carried you for miles, and have appreciation for your grandmother's dishes that will now serve someone who truly needs them.*

If you're challenged, here are some recommendations:

- *Decide what you'd replenish.* If there was a fire and you only got X number of dollars from the insurance company, what would you replace? Or, if you were honest, what would you be relieved was gone? If you had to move, what would you pay to move to your next home? Ask yourself these questions and see if anything is easier to release.

- *Box it up and write a date.* With goods that you're on the fence about relinquishing, store and write the date on top. If you don't use/want/need any of the items in six months, let them go. The key is to just donate the box and not open it back up because there's a good chance it will morph into clutter again.

- *Create a shadow box/collage/quilt or something creative.* Figure out how to honor the items that have memories and that are important to you. There are many ideas on Pinterest to inspire you to celebrate your memories and many talented people on Etsy or other places who can create unique ways to respect what you choose to keep. Be discerning though about what truly means something to you and/or is really useful.

- *Take pictures.* Make a book of photos that you can print or keep on your computer. You might discover in a year or two that some of your possessions really don't hold a lot of memories for you anymore and you can recycle the book or delete the pictures.

- *Ask yourself if someone can get better use.* Would someone appreciate and want to be gifted the possession(s)? Ask friends and family what they would like with a firm deadline to choose and pick up within two weeks. If no one wants anything, donate.

*Theresa had a basement full of boxes and knickknacks that belonged to her parents. For over 20 years the boxes sat in her basement and were never opened. Even though they were out of sight, the boxes were never out of Theresa's mind. It was as if there was a constant drip drip drip at the back of her head. Just walking by the basement door made Theresa feel guilty and exhausted. She was overwhelmed with a sense that she had let her parents down by not using what they left behind, picking up her mother's sewing hobby, or finding a way to honor her father's wonderful ability to fix anything with all the tools he owned.*

*As we worked through some of the boxes, I suggested to her that she wasn't taking into account that her physical clutter was costing her big time mentally and emotionally. This made Theresa pause and really understand what all these boxes were doing to her overall health. She acknowledged that her parents would want her to be happy and would be embarrassed that their possessions had become a burden.*

*When Theresa finally let go of all the boxes of junk she didn't want, she was able to create a space that embraced all of her hobbies. She is even talking of starting a business with her creative endeavors. Talk about enriching your life!*

Look back at your list of **what clutter is truly costing you** that you created at the beginning of the book. Peace of mind? Money to store goods never used or to replace items you already own but can't find in your clutter? Time spent searching for what you need?

Emotional energy of feeling drained every time you walk by the room or into the house? Spiritual clutter because you don't have a space where you can create and grow? Be really honest and understand the true cost. I think you'll be surprised to discover that you're losing more than you may realize.

When going through belongings that have an emotional charge, I suggest **tackling them at a time when you are most energized.** Get support as someone who is neutral and not attached to your possessions can offer valuable help. Allow yourself time to process, grieve, and cherish any goods that you're letting go.

I worked with a client who had lost a child. Understandably, it took her several years before she was able to let go of her child's crib. After she had done a lot of grieving and realized that a child in need could use the crib, she was able to let it go and move forward. To honor her child's memory, she created a shadow box of clothes, toys, and books that both she and her little girl had loved.

I want to be clear that I'm not saying, "Get rid of all your memories!" Separate the wheat from the chaff and hold on to what is truly important and not the stuff that has become clutter in your space, heart, and head.

<u>Summary</u>
Your memories are in your head and heart, not in material goods. Keep only the items with recollections that you truly love and find a way to honor them.

# → Take Actions:

- Write down all of the paraphernalia you're holding on to because of the past.
- Contemplate memories being in your head and heart and record how that feels.
- Go through possessions that have special meaning and release what you can.
- Ask family or friends what they would like. Give them a two-week deadline and donate what they don't choose.
- Decide how you'll honor the items you choose to keep.
- Begin any projects to honor the objects you're keeping.
- Honor and cherish important belongings moving forward.

# Chapter 4

## After the Holidays

*Holidays can be an opportunity to release not only material possessions but also gain closure.*

Our holiday elements can have a lot of emotions attached to them and that can mean you wind up with a lot more stuff that you fail to declutter year after year. You might think that people would only hold on to accouterments that elicited happy feelings, but I've found the opposite can be true. Sometimes people hold on to belongings that may bring up shame, guilt, or sadness. Many of us spend time with families during the holidays and it doesn't mean that it's always joyful.

*When Celeste's mother died, she left Celeste her nutcracker collection. Dutifully, Celeste would put out the nutcrackers, one by one, each and every year. But they didn't bring her any happiness or comfort. Instead she began to feel irritated and burdened. The nutcrackers no longer held joyous memories of her mother and instead reminded Celeste of all their conflicts and what drove her crazy about her mother.*

*I explained to Celeste that she wasn't dishonoring her mother by not wanting to have hundreds of nutcrackers displayed. We went through the large collection and she chose to keep only the nutcrackers that really meant something to her such as an "artist" nutcracker because her mother was a painter. She was able to give some of the nutcrackers to family and then she donated the rest.*

*Now, when Celeste displays the few nutcrackers she kept, she feels wonderful and they conjure up all the wonderful times she shared with her mother. She experiences delight every time she looks at them.*

## Tackling Clutter

Clearing your clutter allows you to **focus on what's important**. It's about learning to flex your discernment muscles. The holidays can be overwhelming because you tend to get many gifts. After the holidays is a great time to purge and start the year off right. You already have all the decorations out (or most of them), so why not take the step to clear out some before you pack them away? I also love decluttering at this time of year because it's usually easy and it gets me mentally prepared to start the New Year off focused.

I suggest starting with gifts. You may receive presents that you don't like and/or additions to your collections that can easily transform into clutter. While bringing in the new, release the old.

What did you get the most of for the holidays? Clothes, books, electronics? Begin decluttering in those areas where you received the majority of your gifts. Consider putting a limit on them i.e. "No more books than can fit in one large bookcase." When you set limits, it gives you a boundary and makes it easier to let go. (Review Chapter 1 for tips on how to declutter.)

If you **received gifts you didn't like, consider donating or giving them away.** As a family, decide what charity you want to give to. Many non-profits have auctions and can use unopened or new gifts. I know some will even take gently used items, but check with the non-profit first. Or you can consider adopting a family. Your local school or church will know who is in need that you can support.

If you have children, I'd encourage you to get them in the habit of decluttering. Now is an especially great time to go through toys, books, movies, stuffed animals, and electronic gadgets.

★*TIP*: *Next holiday season, ask for what you really desire and be as specific as possible. Many times people are relieved that you're making gift giving easier. Also, when you give a gift, give it with zero expectation that the recipient will keep, use, or love.*

While you're decluttering gifts, I encourage you to **create a gift shelf**. A gift shelf is an easy place to store gifts. As someone who shops for the holidays year round to save time and money, my gift shelf enables me to easily see what I have and who I have already purchased gifts for. I also like to keep random unwrapped items here for hostess gifts and in case I need to unexpectedly provide a gift.

First, **find a place to store your gifts**. It could be under a bed, a linen closet, or a shelf in a guest room. Remember to think about what you're storing. The garage is exposed to the elements and probably not the best place to keep presents.

Boxes and bins of **uniform size make it easy to stack and store**. Most of us are visual, so you may choose to create a system that is color-coded e.g., immediate family in the blue bin, hostess gifts in the purple bin, spouse in the red bin, etc.

Keep **track of all your items on the gift shelf with some type of inventory.** At the beginning of the year I create separate lists for people and occasions. For each person: gift ideas, sizes, hobbies, and <u>monetary limit</u>. Don't forget the monetary limit! So many people wake up with credit card hangover in January. With planning, you can prevent a huge bill after the holidays. I also like to keep track of what I buy people each year, so I have a list of gifts and won't repeat.

I also keep regifts in the same area, but make sure I write down who gave me the present. You don't want a Seinfeld moment and give back a gift to the original gift giver. I also make sure to not regift within the same group of friends or family.

★*TIP: Keep a master gift list in your purse or wallet or on an app on your phone or tablet. You never know when you'll see the perfect present. You can also put reminders in your calendar for gifts you need to buy that month.*

<u>Decorations</u>
Is that you saying, "Wow! I didn't know I had this many decorations?" When you haven't decluttered in a while, stuff can pile up. Also, with something like seasonal items that are packed away, you may not realize how much you've accumulated, especially if holiday items are located in different parts of your home.

Begin by **locating <u>every</u> decoration**, whether you use or not. Comb through each room, closet, outside storage, basement, attic, etc. Once you gather everything, lay them out in one room or area. This is a great visual to show you just how much you really have. Seeing it in one area, as opposed to spread throughout the house and yard, may surprise you with how much you actually own.

Now **go through and categorize all of your decorations:** ornaments, lights, stockings, entertainment, etc. Sort however it makes the most sense to you. Think about what you would label a box if you were going to retrieve it. What category pops into your mind? We celebrate Christmas in my household, so <u>tree</u> is one of my categories and includes ornaments, beads, and lights. Someone else may prefer to categorize those decorations as <u>ornaments</u>. Take the time to decide and make it easier on yourself when it comes time to pull out everything next season.

Once you separate your decorations into categories, go through each category one by one. What can you release? Do you still like or love? Would a friend or family member appreciate them more?

Can you **look to the natural world for decorations** to release some of what you own? Add pinecones or garlands to the mantle? Thread popcorn and cranberries on the tree? Decorate with ginger bread houses? With places like Pinterest and YouTube you can get really creative and have a lot of fun.

Try and **be realistic about what you're no longer using or what brings you joy.** Once you edit each category, I encourage you to go through your "keep" donations again, especially if you didn't let go of a lot.

You may love and use everything and that is okay. People get tripped up when they love everything (books, cd's, holiday, etc.) and it becomes way too much. If holidays are your favorite time of year and you love hundreds of nutcrackers, go for it! But if you see a decoration that brings your energy down or makes you melancholy, your best bet is to let it go.

Once you have your purge pile, decide if you would like to sell, donate, give to family or friends, put on an app like *LetGo*, or have a garage sale. If you aren't going to get the item(s) out of the house immediately, place in boxes or bags, label, and keep out of the way in a closet, basement, or garage. Make sure boxes are packed properly if they'll be exposed to the elements and bags are tightly sealed.

With the decorations you're keeping, pack into containers and label. I love to color coordinate bins if I have them. I have a few bins that are red and green that I use for Christmas.

Finally, **make a master inventory list of what you own**. Post or keep it near where you store decorations, on your computer or app, or in a master holiday file. If you do a really effective purge, you don't need to go through holiday items every year, but I'd encourage you to go through your decorations every few years at minimum.

★*TIP: Drink wine and clear clutter. I repurpose boxes from the wine store. Those cases protect 12 bottles of wine and I trust them to keep my ornaments and other holiday items safe. Sometimes I have been able to color coordinate the boxes i.e. red for Christmas. Most wine stores will give you boxes even if you don't purchase wine.*

## Cards

This is another great area to go through that you might not have thought of, especially if you like to keep cards past the holiday season. I have had clients who have had <u>thousands</u> of cards in boxes that they hadn't looked at in years; they couldn't remember some of the people. That's a lot of cards taking up a lot of space.

Now, don't think I'm against cards; I keep cards my husband gives me, but I go through everything else with a fine toothcomb. I went through our engagement and wedding cards and kept only a handful. They were ones that meant a lot to us from people with whom we are close. My mom also paints the card she and my father send out each holiday season. I will one day have them all professionally framed.

I always encourage my clients to go through everything they own each year. The more you do it the easier it becomes. If you don't declutter for years, you wind up with a backlog of work. Regular maintenance prevents that.

★*TIP:* *If you love giving cards, consider these alternatives that won't create card clutter:*

- https://www.paperlesspost.com/cards/section/online-cards
- http://www.birthdayalarm.com/
- https://www.e-cards.com/
- https://www.bluemountain.com/
- https://www.jacquielawson.com/

- https://www.punchbowl.com/ecards

## Gift Wrap

Gift-wrap is something that can also create a lot of mess. I encourage you to really go through, edit, and donate. See if there is a reuse store, Girl Scout troop, or a local classroom that can use extra paper. Again, if this is your passion and you love to wrap gifts for every occasion (I had a customer who had St. Patrick's Day paper!) then go for it. Again, be honest with yourself about how many possessions you're claiming are very important.

★*TIP:* *Look for giftwrap with a high post-consumer recycled content as paper that avoids cutting down trees and closes the recycling loop.*

To lighten your gift-wrap load, here are some ideas.

- *Choose your one-of-a-kind colors.* Perhaps you choose red, silver, and white. These colors by themselves can work with any holiday. I love purple and turquoise. Depending on the occasion, you can use different colored ribbon.
- *Consider reusable Wrapsacks.* When you give the gift, tell the recipient to reuse the Wrapsack.
- *Reuse giftwrap.* Sometimes the paper is in good enough condition and you can reuse. My mother has saved and reused ribbons since I was a child. You can also cut up holiday cards and repurpose them as gift tags.
- *Get creative.* Use magazines, catalogs, or newspaper as gift-wrap. Butcher-block paper looks great with some twine or a pretty ribbon. Let children decorate, and personalize.

- *As part of the gift.* Use a pail if you're gifting to the gardener, a loaf pan to the baker or a toolbox for the handyman to hold your gifts and serve as wrapping paper.

Summary
After the holidays is a great time to declutter as you most likely have most of your holiday accouterments displayed, categorized, and separated. Save a step by decluttering before you put it all away.

→ Take Actions:

- Declutter any area where you received many gifts.
- Decide if you'd like to donate any gifts to a charity.
- Create a gift shelf.
- Make a master gift list for all the presents you'll need the following year.
- Purge decorations and decide whether to sell, donate, or give away.
- Sort through holiday cards. Release the ones that aren't important.
- Get rid of excess gift-wrap.

# Chapter 5

## The Junk Drawer

*What you tell yourself you become.*

Most of us have at least one junk drawer, if not more. Many of us have junk drawers in the kitchen, but I have also seen them in the garage, basement, attic, bathroom, office, and bedroom.

A blog post from the now defunct ShareSpace.com[4] found that the average American has credit card debt of $15,185 and around $7,000 of unwanted junk collecting dust. It's also estimated that $15 billion in unused tech gadgets are in junk drawers worldwide. That amounts to $2,200 per drawer. How much money do you think is sitting in your drawer(s)?

*John had junk drawers that became his Achilles heal. He was pretty clutter free throughout the rest of his home, but when it came to this one small area, he was out of control. As we talked, John revealed to me that his dad used to tinker a lot. Their junk drawers had consisted mainly of broken bits and pieces—a wheel from a toy truck, rusted scissors, and his mother's warped hair ties. What others saw as junk, John's father saw as a way to experiment and have fun. All those scraps and pieces could be made into something if they just had a chance.*

*To John, the junk drawer represented a way to connect with his deceased father. We talked about other ways he could feel close to his father. After we cleared out the junk drawers, we created a space in his garage to tinker. This brought out the little boy in John because we created groups of items such as "monsters", "space travel", and "the world's next greatest invention." These were topics he and his father had spent hours discussing.*

*The junk drawers have disappeared from John's house. He spends time in his creative area weekly. It serves not only a way to connect with his father, but also to unwind and unleash his imagination. When John honored what his soul needed, he was able to release his clutter.*

## Releasing the Miscellaneous

I love the junk drawer because it's **something you can usually easily clear and gain a sense of accomplishment.** It's a "win win" because you get to declutter, you can do it quickly, and reap an immediate reward. If you're new to decluttering, this is a great way to start flexing your clutter busting muscles.

If you're someone with more than one of these catchall drawers, can you get all of them decluttered?

The first crucial step: **create a new name.** Begin by renaming your junk drawer. Completely remove "junk drawer" from your vocabulary. It's so easy to clutter it up because you've already declared everything in it is worthless. You tell yourself it's okay to throw crap in it because that's its purpose. Turn off the autopilot on referring to it as the junk drawer. I'm not a fan of calling it the miscellaneous drawer either because it effortlessly becomes a catchall. You tend to become lazy if there's a free for all drawer where you can just throw something in it and forget about it.

Come up with a better name. Coraccio Fix It. Seibert Problem Solver. Julie's Mail Center. You get the idea. If you name the drawer something you like, you're most likely going to put what fits into that category. Keep the name broad, so you have some leeway. If it doesn't fit in that group, then it's a good indication it belongs with other like items in another location. You most likely already have a home for pens, stamps, or matches.

Once you create your brand new name, it's time to declutter.

First, you'll want to **empty everything out of the drawer**. I suggest putting all of the knickknacks on some tea or dishtowels you can throw in the laundry right after you finish. Take the time to give the drawer a good dusting or use a damp paper towel or dust cloth to clean out.

Release, and if possible recycle, the real junk. What is "real junk"? It's expired anything, such as coupons. Put the dried up pens out of their misery.[5] Let go of the broken paraphernalia, too, such as half pencils, candle nubs, bent paperclips and binder clips, eraser chunks, unused mail labels, or useless batteries.

Return goods that belong in other homes, such as cards with games, stamps with bills, or matches in your emergency kit.

After you declutter, **group the remaining elements** how it makes sense to you. See suggestions in Chapter 1 if you need support categorizing. What's most important is that it makes sense to you. I suggest having what you use frequently for easy access. If you pay bills at the kitchen table, you'll want stamps, checkbooks, envelopes, and pens in the drawer.

Once you've pared down the drawer, returned items, and chosen your categories, spend a few minutes organizing. I don't have any special dividers or containers in the Coraccio Fix It drawer. We don't have a lot of knickknacks here—pens, paper, and mail slips mainly.

If you can **easily sift through and find what you need**, you should be okay. I'm a fan of not creating unnecessary work or buying containers when I don't need them. If you have odd shaped knickknacks or lots of different odds and ends, here are some ideas with things you most likely already have:

- Zip Lock Baggies are clear and you can easily label with a sharpie.
- Recycle check boxes to hold materials. Use square or rectangular boxes to maximize space in your drawer.
- Small snack containers or reusable silicone bags can hold pushpins, paperclips, stamps, etc.

If it's important to you to be very organized, you can find small containers to fit in your drawer or use drawer dividers.

Don't forget to **do regular maintenance** on the drawer. You'll need to be diligent here as this area can easily get out of hand. Spend ten minutes or less one Saturday a month clearing clutter or 20 minutes or so quarterly and you should be okay. Do this while your coffee is brewing, in between loads of laundry, or while listening to your favorite podcast, *Clear Your Clutter Inside & Out.*

★*TIP*: *If you're storing loose 9-volt, AA, AAA, or other batteries in a drawer in your home, watch how you store them. Don't store them loose and rolling around with other metals, glues, and other knickknacks.*

It doesn't take much to heat a metallic object or cause a spark and start a fire. A Brillo pad, aluminum foil, or a paper clip can short out on a 9-volt battery. A 9-volt battery is a fire hazard because the positive and negative posts are on top, right next to one another. When storing any of your batteries, place in a small box, plastic container, or bag. I recommend using the package the battery came in. Don't let them roll around freely.

When you dispose or recycle batteries, wrap in electrical tape or something to keep separated from anything else that may come in contact with it. If you aren't clearing your formerly-called the junk drawer soon, please check your batteries immediately.

Summary
Decluttering your formerly-known as the junk drawer is usually easy and a quick win to get your clutter busting muscles going.

→ Take Actions:

- Rename the junk drawer(s).
- Toss and recycle the real junk.
- Clean out the drawer(s).

- Categorize what goes back into the drawer.
- Return items that belong somewhere else.
- Find dividers or repurpose items to contain what's left.
- Containerize in a plastic bag or box any loose batteries.
- Wrap batteries when disposing or recycling in electrical tape.

# MENTAL

A cluttered mind has obsessive, unsettled, or repetitive thoughts. For some, it feels like your mind controls you or there is no "off" button. Most of us experience mental clutter or "monkey mind" daily. For others it may be reinforcing negative concepts about yourself, staying stuck in unhealthy self-talk, or replaying events or moments from the past. Perhaps you spin your wheels trying to solve others' problems, not checking in about where you are in life, or being completely overwhelmed with too many thoughts competing for attention in your head.

What's your mental clutter? Do you have obsessive thoughts? Ruminate on what you should have said? Are you always thinking about business? Do you spend hours picking something apart? What else may be causing you mental clutter that you haven't acknowledged?

As you clear your mental clutter pay attention. Do you become motivated to release physical objects? Are you able to stay calm because your mind is clear? Can you connect more easily with your spirit and soul because your mind isn't cluttered?

# Clearing your mind allows you to hear your inner voice.

# Chapter 6

## Past, Present, or Future?

*Your point of power to change is in the present moment.*

For most of my life I wrote New Year's resolutions. I started in December so I was ready to tackle everything January 1st. I designed a colorful poster to focus and be inspired. How wonderful that I could have a new beginning each year! I was so excited for what I'd achieve that year. Unfortunately, my beautiful poster would be in the recycling bin within a few months because it had become a burden, and worse, a reminder I wasn't accomplishing what I set out to do. I'd be filled with guilt and then feel like a failure. I lost steam and motivation and then waited until the next January 1st to start anew.

I learned a "secret" that has not only helped me to be happier, but also has empowered me: **in every moment we have the choice to start fresh.** Most of us spend the majority of our time living in the past or the future. You're unaware of that because you're on autopilot and have been functioning this way for so long. When you focus on the past or the future how can you expect to change your life?

This realization that each moment gives you an opportunity to start fresh allows you to no longer be held hostage or be controlled by your past or future. How many times do you dwell on the past (*If only I said...*) or worry about the future (*What if this relationship doesn't work out?*)? You lose your power when you're anywhere but the present. When you live in the present moment, it truly is a gift.

*Marcy was always living in the past when it came to her relationships. She would brood about the relationships that failed, the man that got away, and the boyfriends who did her wrong. When Marcy focused her energy on her past relationships, she couldn't see all the available men right in front of her.*

*As we talked, I gently suggested to Marcy that perhaps focusing her attention on her past relationships was a way to avoid the potential pain of a new relationship not working out. She started to cry and said that she was worried about being rejected. "What if it doesn't work out and I wind up alone again?"*

*Marcy began addressing her fears by letting go of her past relationships. She did a healing ceremony for each man that included thanking each one for what he had taught her. Next, Marcy became present with her fear. To combat her loneliness, she began to volunteer at an animal sanctuary. Marcy became happier, felt less alone, and focused less on having to find a relationship. Being happy and present attracted a lot of suitors and she is currently having a ball dating.*

*Rhea, on the other hand, experienced great anxiety about the future. She worried about having enough money for retirement. Rhea would read all the doom and gloom predictions and that only added to her anxiety. She was paralyzed with fear and could easily spiral down with worry that she would end up homeless.*

*We talked about how Rhea could create her future, and reduce her anxiety, by living in the present. When she was in the moment, and not hanging out years in the future, Rhea could create a plan for retirement. We brainstormed different ideas that she could implement. We broke each item down into manageable steps, so Rhea didn't feel overwhelmed. She began to feel more in control and her anxiety eased.*

*Because she was less stressed, Rhea thought clearly and began to make strides in saving for retirement. While she still occasionally panics, she knows to bring herself present and focus on a step she can take right then to ease her mind.*

### Where Am I?

Are you living in the past, present, or future? Do you tend to get stuck in the same topics again and again? Where do you spend most of your mental energy? You might be amazed at **how much time you're living in the past or future**. Once you're aware, you can make changes.

As for the barrage of thoughts that enter your mind, don't judge them or try to change them. Be a bystander and observe. For example, you see someone who is poised and confident and think, "I'll never be like that." Pause and take a deep breath. Try saying to yourself, "Wow, isn't that interesting? I wonder why I said that to myself?" The goal here is to increase your self-awareness without judgment.

The first time I did this exercise I thought I was going to go crazy. I considered myself a positive person mainly living in the present. I discovered I was fairly negative because I was mainly focused on the past. It was important that I didn't beat myself up for focusing on the past. I could have easily gone down the rabbit hole of the laundry list of what I thought I did wrong. I encourage you, too, to begin practicing staying present by focusing on the fact that you're making changes and moving forward. Be gentle with yourself.

★*TIP*: *Try this exercise while engaged in a physical activity. I do this while mowing the lawn. Some other possibilities include while washing dishes, painting your nails, or folding clothes.*

Become aware of your thoughts. You can choose to do this for a few minutes, hours, day, a few days, or a week or two. Whatever you're comfortable doing, as there is no set timetable. What's important is **figuring out where you're spending your time.** This is where writing down your thoughts and keeping a journal can be very helpful.

EXAMPLES:

*During a work meeting my thoughts drifted to my last job where I wish I had stood up to my boss who treated me unfairly.*

*On a date with Steve I found myself wondering if he was the one.*

*In my bubble bath I was really present—smelling the bubbles, feeling the warmth of the water, and enjoying the moment.*

*At Starbuck's I found myself worrying about having enough money for my retirement after I calculated I spend $50 weekly on coffee.*

When you find yourself drifting to the past or future, become present with a quick and easy exercise:

- Wear a beaded bracelet and say an "I am" statement.
- Set your phone or watch to alert you at certain times each day so that when you hear the signal, you'll stop, take a deep breath, and observe what you're thinking and feeling.
- Do a quick body scan and check in to see how different parts of your body are feeling.
- Activate your senses and notice five things you can see, four items you can feel, three things you can hear, two things you can smell and one thing you can taste.
- Walk mindfully at a natural pace. Pay attention to all of your sensations as you walk. Involve all five of your senses. Keep an open awareness as you walk and engage your body.

Will you always be present? Of course not! But you are building your "be present" muscles. The more you do this the easier it becomes. The more present you are the more you can make choices that will create your future.

Try and learn more about yourself. **Can you understand why your thoughts may be in the past or future?** If you think about the past, wishing you'd responded differently, do you need better boundaries or to speak up for yourself going forward? If you find your mind wandering to the future, what can you do <u>right now</u> to alleviate worries? What can you do <u>right now</u> that will support you in creating the future you desire?

After you gain some awareness, dig a little deeper. Continue to journal your responses. You can also do some meditative or free flow writing and see what comes up. Simply set a timer for 15 minutes, ask yourself a question, and write. Don't try to focus on an answer. You may have an answer come in a roundabout way.

## EXAMPLES:

*I noticed I'm afraid I'll never be a mother. I'm single and not getting any younger. It's really expensive to freeze your eggs and I'm not sure I want to go through that. I have all this nurturing energy and I need to do something with that. I'm not interested in babysitting but maybe I could offer to dog sit for Mary and see if maybe I'd like to get a pet. Just thinking about having someone else at home calms me. Maybe it's more my loneliness I need to worry about now instead of going so far into the future.*

*I found myself obsessing about my friendship with Suzie. That makes no sense. Why would I waste all this time thinking about her? As I'm looking back at the past few times we've spent together, I realize she talks about herself and rarely asks about me. She seems to only call when she needs something from me. Maybe I'm spending so much time thinking about this because I need to speak up about how I feel or spend less time with her. Hmmmm. I've been concerned if our friendship ends then I won't have any close friends. Who needs a friend like Suzie? I'm going to register for a women's event I saw and see if I can forge new friendships.*

What came up? Did anything surprise you? What jumps out that you'd like to change? Do you see how any of these mind games create mental clutter?

Review your journal. Choose one area of your life or a habitual thought you'd like to change. What can you do in the present moment to ease your mind? Can you replace it with a positive thought or take an action?

Write down your thought and create an action plan to change it.

## EXAMPLE:

**Area/Thought:** *I worry about not having enough money when I retire.*

**My Plan:**
1. *Ask friends who are good at managing money how they save and seek recommendations for a financial advisor.*
2. *Start contributing to my company's retirement fund.*
3. *Quit cable T.V. and go with a less expensive option, then put the extra money in a mutual fund.*
4. *Create a budget and stick to it.*
5. *Do one extra mortgage payment a year to pay off the house early.*

As you become more present, and continue to monitor your thoughts, you can see how being in the present empowers you to make choices and take action. When you're in the past or future you spin your wheels and stay stuck.

Summary
The present is your point of power to change. Become more present each day and consciously create your life.

→ Take Actions:

- Monitor and record your thoughts.
- Recognize if you're mainly in the past, present, or future.
- Examine and learn from your thoughts and beliefs.
- Choose an exercise to bring you back to the present when you find yourself drifting to the past or future.
- Create a plan to release any concerns taking you out of the present moment.
- Address persistent thoughts that keep you stuck in the past or pulled into the future.

# Chapter 7

## The Just Becauses

*Just because you've always done something doesn't mean you must continue.*

If I'm honest, I've been plagued by the "just becauses" the majority of my life. One of the advantages of aging, is that it's easier to let what doesn't matter go, chose what you'd like to do, and not buy into what other people would like you to do.

My mind would work overtime with people I would be worried I'd let down, the ones who would be angry with me, and let's not forget people who would go into guilt trip overdrive. Once I began to really examine why I was doing something, and if it was truly for me and my family, I began to unravel the expectations and the requirements of the "just becauses". **Talk about feeling free!**

*I was fortunate to grow up in a small town with the majority of my family (grandparents, cousins, aunts, uncles) living in the immediate area. My mother's family was about 90 minutes away and others within driving distance on the east coast.*

*Because everyone is near, we spent holidays together and still do. My grandmother, Janice Seibert, was our awesome matriarch and she set certain rules. Holiday dinners required us to dress up and were formal. This was important to my grandmother because she wanted us to learn how to behave on a formal occasion and learn how to use all the appropriate utensils. Some women in our town had been pointedly unkind to her and it was important to Janice that her children and grandchildren were never shut out because of lack of manners. My grandmother wanted us to feel equally comfortable dining with paupers as well as millionaires.*

*My parents and aunts have continued the tradition of dressing up and having a formal dinner.[6] My husband and I live in North Carolina, so we aren't always able to get home for the holidays. Tony, my husband, spends almost every year working on Thanksgiving. If he gets Thanksgiving off, he must work Christmas. Because of this, we've created our own traditions.*

*We had no desire for something formal and opted to keep it casual. Tony is Italian and I love anything associated with Italy so I usually cook a dish that is from a region where his parents immigrated from for Christmas dinner.*

*It was tough at first because I had celebrated the other traditions for over 40 years. I wondered what my grandmother would think. Would she be disappointed? How about my parents? Was I not respecting my family's traditions and values? How would Tony's parents feel about a non-Italian taking over the cooking? Would everyone be upset? Would I be shunned?*

*In the middle of my crazy thought process, I stopped and took a deep breath. And then I had to give myself the advice that I always give to others. When people have passed they want you to be happy. I also believe that those alive choose for us to not be burdened by their choices. They might not always agree with our decisions, but, in the end, they do desire us to be content. One of the plus sides of being an adult is choosing how to celebrate the holidays.*

Cooking Italian makes me happy and I do it every year we don't go to West Virginia for the holidays. Instead of feeling burdened by doing things that aren't special for me, I'm energized with celebrating how my husband and I choose. It's fun for me to find new recipes and I've really enjoyed expanding my culinary skills.

You can also have the "just becauses" in relationships. I had a friend, Josie, I had known almost 40 years. Throughout our friendship, Josie would pout, criticize and insult me regularly, and shared with my parents mean comments people said about me in high school.

The final straw for me was when I posted my engagement on Facebook and Josie snidely remarked, "WOW! That was fast!" I deleted her comment and unfollowed her. I had remained friends with her *just because* we had been friends for so long and because I had loved her father. However, I realized in that moment that a relationship with her was unhealthy for me. It was time to cut the cord. When you know what's important you can clear relationship clutter. (This is on the list for the next volume of *Clear Your Clutter Inside & Out*.)

*Miriam came from a long line of Miriam's. The first-born daughter was to be named Miriam Phillipa. Miriam wasn't a fan of her name because she felt it wasn't truly hers; she shared it with the twelve other Miriam's. When she found out she was pregnant with her daughter, she didn't want to continue the tradition. However, she really struggled with breaking a long-standing practice.*

*One night, she shared her feelings with her mother. Much to her surprise, and relief, her mother, known as Mimi, agreed with her decision not to name her granddaughter Miriam Phillipa. Mimi shared how she wanted to name Miriam the Italian name of Annina in honor of her husband's heritage but she got a lot of pressure and resistance from her family. She vowed that if Miriam ever had a daughter she wouldn't guilt her into continuing the tradition just because several generations had done so. While the name Annina didn't resonate with Miriam, she did name a cat they rescued after her mother's favorite name. Now Mimi not only has a beautiful granddaughter, Emma, she also has a grand kitty Annina who are both equally spoiled.*

Examining your "just becauses" doesn't mean you have to end a relationship or start or stop a new tradition. It can mean that you need to discuss boundaries with a friend or family member, or change a pattern that doesn't help either of you, or maybe you need to say no when a friend asks you to volunteer for an organization you don't choose to support.

### Dealing with the "Just Becauses"
The Holidays are a great time to examine why you do something "just because." No matter if you celebrate Christmas, Chanukah, Kwanza, or Winter Solstice, you more than likely have experienced some of these situations. When you identify those situations, **you can reassess what really matters to *you* and then make decisions that support your priorities and who you are *now*.** Holidays can be especially challenging as you bump up against traditions.

Do you see yourself in any of the following examples?

*You buy gifts for everyone in your extended family just because that's how it's always been, but spending money you don't have leaves you stressed out, in debt, and you're not even sure anyone likes or needs the gifts you buy.*

*Aunt Maple will be upset if you don't have a slice of her world famous triple chocolate pumpkin pie just because she toiled all day in the kitchen, but you're committed to eating healthier and not going completely overboard during the holidays.*

*You really want to slow down and savor the season but just because you've always gone to your neighbors' open house you feel obligated to go again, despite the fact that your neighbors leave you exhausted and drained.*

Here are some priorities my clients have had:

- No debt from giving gifts.
- Not spending time with people that they don't like or with whom they're not close.
- Not going overboard eating everything in sight.
- Not having a jam-packed schedule.
- Creating new joyful traditions.
- Maintaining healthy habits.
- Simplifying the holidays.

Do any of these resonate with you?

**What are your priorities?** I'm a huge fan of writing down because it has helped so many of my clients. Whether you write in a journal, sketchpad, or app, it helps so much to put it down in black and white. I encourage you to have one place where you write everything down. If you do, you can easily reference your thoughts. Scattered notes in numerous places won't do you a lot of good and it will only add to visual clutter.

**Seeing your priorities and easily referencing them** can help make them stick. Of course, they can be adjusted, but you're more likely to get what you need to have done when you write your goals and to-dos down. Crossing something off or deleting an item from a list gives you a sense of accomplishment.

Reflect on what's important to you for this holiday season. **What's most meaningful to you <u>right now</u>?** Maybe you need to take a nap, exercise, or eat a healthy meal. What will reduce your stress and bring you peace of mind? Making a list of what you choose not to do, whether it's buying fewer gifts, or volunteering instead of entertaining. Who else needs to be involved in the decision-making? Spouse, children, or friends?

<u>Try This Exercise</u>

Make a list of what you enjoyed about past holidays.
      "Making gingerbread houses with the family."
      "Baking homemade cookies and pies."
      "Going to church and hearing the choir sing."

Don't forget to also record what you didn't like.

      "Attending the office holiday party."
      "Buying gifts for a dozen family members."
      "Gaining five pounds."

Have some fun and dream about what you might enjoy trying during the holiday season on a third list.

"Sledding."
"Flying to NYC for New Year's Eve."
"Celebrating with my closest friends."
"A cabin in the mountains for a week of solitude."

Remember, **you *always* have a choice**! If you find yourself complaining that you don't have a choice, that isn't true. Doing nothing is a choice. Even if you feel someone railroaded you in to doing something, you still made a choice to allow it. Knowing you have a choice empowers you to make the right decision for you.

Here are some areas where I've seen my clients get overwhelmed and fall back on the "just becauses." I've also included some possible solutions.

*Overspending.* Have you ever wakened in January to a credit card hangover along with a diminished bank account? Spending more than you can afford not only can create stress but also cause bigger problems if you go into debt or extend your credit.

Potential Solutions: **Have a conversation with family and friends about gifts and spending.** See how they feel about gift giving. Some might think the same way as you do and will be relieved you suggested! Years ago, I stopped exchanging gifts with my brothers. A few years after that, we had a conversation to reduce the number of gifts among extended family. The generation above gives gifts to the generations below. So, I receive gifts from my parents and aunts and give gifts to my nieces and nephew and cousin.

As we get older, it's usually a little easier to trim our gift-giving list. Someone might get upset, but honestly, if someone emphasizes receiving gifts, how important is the relationship?

Whatever you do, don't forget to keep a running budget so you don't overspend.

*Anxiety about gift giving and receiving.* You worry about not choosing the right gift and the last thing you want to do is create clutter for someone else.

Possible Solutions: Be proactive and **ask what people desire** or use these ideas:

- Buy experiences. You can buy concert or play tickets, a gift certificate to a themed restaurant, or a daytime excursion.
- Donate to a charity that the gift recipient supports in his or her honor.
- Give memberships to a gym or club.
- Make your own gifts: bath salts or soap, all the ingredients for soup or cake, or essential oil perfumes.
- Offer your babysitting, gardening, or culinary services.

What other ideas can you discover?

ⓘ **IMPORTANT NOTE:** *Please think through giving pets as gifts. While I'm a huge animal advocate and know* *that so many cats and dogs need homes, proceed with extreme caution. If you're buying a pet for someone consider their lifestyle, financial ability, and the time and love they have to give to a pet. There's nothing worse for the pet (and the human) than having to return him or her to the rescue or shelter.*

*Overindulging and overextending yourself.* It can be with eating or entertaining, and regretting it before, during, and after! Have you gained five or ten pounds each season? How many times have you been exhausted from your time off because you didn't get any rest because of a packed schedule?

Possible Solutions: This is a great time to **start a self-care routine** if you don't have one already: book a massage, commit to a nightly bubble bath, have your hair styled, or indulge in a manicure.

Find an accountability buddy who can help you stick to moderation when scheduling events or going through the buffet at the party. **Say <u>no</u> to what you don't want to do and stick to it.** Plan what you'd like to do and include time for rest and relaxation. Serve appetizers instead of an elaborate meal. Volunteer at a soup kitchen or a charity. Go out to eat so you can concentrate on spending time with family and friends instead of shopping, cooking, and serving for days. If you don't have the funds to go out, invite friends over for a potluck.

**Do something you desire instead of being sucked into pressure, guilt, or a knee jerk reaction.** The holidays should be about connecting, celebrating, being grateful, and your religious or spiritual beliefs, not about Black Friday deals, feeling overwhelmed, and running around like crazy.

Did any of the examples I give ring true? What were you thinking about as you were reading? If there were no rules and no one was watching, what would you choose to do?

I also encourage you to **reflect upon your "just becauses."** Why do you choose to continuing doing them? **What has prevented you from stopping?** Are you concerned you'll upset someone? If you take the time to contemplate, you can sometimes find out that your "just becauses" take away from your life and keep you from exploring other options that can make you happier.

As I mentioned earlier in the chapter, at first I was hesitant about not having a formal holiday dinner as I felt it would show a lack of respect for my grandmother whom I loved dearly. When I took the time to really think about it, I knew that wasn't true. My grandmother always wanted me to be happy. Now, I love cooking my Italian meal.

★*TIP: I do something called* Take It Down *(original title, I know, but sometimes simplicity is the best.) When I have a fear, I write down the worst thing that can happen. When I see it written down, I know that it isn't likely to come to pass. I then say, "What's the next worse thing that can happen?" I continue to take it down to something minute that I know I can handle. Consider whittling your fears to something that's truly realistic. How can you handle it? Who can support you? Many times you're much tougher than you believe and can navigate most of what life throws you. If you have a plan in place, you're even more prepared for the expected or the unexpected.*

While I always love the holidays as a great example of the "just becauses", we have them in everyday life, too. Examine another area in your life where you do something because you always have done it that way.

- *Just because* you have always been the peacemaker in the family doesn't mean you need to continue.
- *Just because* you are the organized one in a marriage doesn't mean you do all the tidying.
- *Just because* you always go to the same place for vacation doesn't mean you can't choose another location.

I think you get the idea.

Like many challenges in life, this is a process. Celebrate where you're able to make changes and commit to making more adjustments in the future.

Summary
Just because you have always done something doesn't mean you're required to continue.

→ Take Actions:

- Write down where you're doing something "just because".
- Reflect upon why you're continuing to do something you don't desire to do.
- Discover what's behind why you continue to do a task that makes you unhappy.

- Choose what you'd like to create and do in place of your "just becauses".
- Eliminate your biggest frustration.
- Continue to be aware of your "just becauses" and release them, as you're able.

# Chapter 8

## When Life Throws a Curveball

*You'll face storms, so learn how to ride the waves.*

I have two friends who went through a divorce. Both had very different processes and results.

*Lisa, while processing her divorce, was able to do some self-reflection and ask, "How did I contribute to the break up of my marriage?" Lisa examined her relationship and her part as to why it ended. Upon contemplation, Lisa realized that she had always been suspicious of her husband cheating, although he was faithful. She would tell him over and over that she didn't trust him. Her lack of trust was a contributing factor to the divorce. Lisa hired a life coach, did a lot of inner work, and took a hard look at her insecurities and actions. It wasn't easy and there was a lot of emotional pain, but Lisa kept working on herself. Because she cleared her inner clutter, when she's in her next relationship, Lisa won't repeat the same mistakes.*

*Self-reflection didn't mean that Lisa wasn't going to be hurt, angry, scared, and sad. Those emotions were part of the process of discovering that her marriage was ending. While she felt and honored all her emotions, she was also able to step back and decide if she wanted to move forward in a haze of rage or steer her ship with as much compassion and understanding for herself as she could.*

*My other friend Carol blamed her husband and took no responsibility in the dissolution of her marriage. To this day, she cries to anyone who will listen, and surrounds herself with people who reinforce the idea that she was wronged and is a victim. Carol has done no inner reflection, even when suggested to do so by those closest to her who truly care about her well-being. She remarried and airs her dirty laundry on social media about her current husband. Guess what? Carol's new husband is just as immature as the first one, albeit in a different way.*

*Getting a divorce can be devastating. In Carol's case she kept picking at and opening her wounds and never allowed herself to heal. Because she spent no time contemplating how she could have negatively contributed to her marriage, Carol sees her new husband at fault for everything. Unless she changes, Carol will most likely be in an unhappy marriage or get divorced again. With some self-awareness she can course correct and have a happy marriage if she chooses. It's all up to her.*

Which woman do you believe has peace in her life, Carol or Lisa? Which woman has learned to ride the wave? Which woman can move forward to have a successful relationship? Which woman would you choose to be?

## Learning to Ride the Waves

You will have experiences that, quite frankly, suck. A few examples in my life include dealing with cruel girls, having my heart broken, being alone, and enduring a mean spirited women's group before I had the courage to leave. When I was in my 20s, a therapist suggested I learn how to ride the waves, instead of crashing every time I experienced unpleasant situations.

The good news is that there are **tools you can use to support you in navigating challenging**

**situations.** The choice is yours whether you learn to ride or crash and burn through life.

*Be honest.* First, don't make a **mountain out of molehill.** Not escalating your problem doesn't diminish what you're going through. Most of us have been fortunate enough to never be hungry, experience being homeless, deal with a life threatening illness, or face a bankruptcy. However, that doesn't mean that what you're going through doesn't sometimes have a huge impact on your life. But the truth is that most of the time, regardless of what happened, your life isn't over, even if you think it is. If you fear you'll never have what you desire, that probably won't be the case. As you grow and change, most likely your desires will grow and change, too. Rarely does one event completely destroy you. There are many stories of people such as Holocaust survivor Elie Wiesel who not only survived suffering in a concentration camp, but learned how to thrive as a political activist, author, and Nobel Laureate, despite enduring something so horrible that most of us have no way of comprehending. You're not out of the game called life.

*Know you don't always know.* You can't see the future and don't know what will happen next. **While something might seem bad, it may not be.**

You might have heard the parable of the Chinese farmer. I have read different versions, but here's a short example.

> *A Chinese farmer gets a horse, which soon runs away. A neighbor says, "That's bad news." The farmer replies, "Good news, bad news, who can say?"*

*The horse comes back and brings another horse with him. Good news, you might say.*

*The farmer gives the second horse to his son, who rides it, then is thrown and badly breaks his leg.*

*"So sorry for your bad news," says the concerned neighbor. "Good news, bad news, who can say?" the farmer replies.*

*In a week or so, the emperor's men come and take every able-bodied young man to fight in a war. The farmer's son is spared.*

*Good news, of course.*

I dated someone on and off for a really long time. I was heartbroken when we finally ended the relationship. If I'm honest, I'm not sure if it was ever realistic, but I chose to hold on to that first real love. However, I had to trust that it wasn't meant to be—and it wasn't. All those other romances that didn't work out were a true blessing. I can look back on my previous relationships and see all that I learned and how I grew into the woman I needed to be to attract my husband.

This was also true of "failed" female friendships. I've had women steal, lie, cheat, and use me. These women taught me self-love, how to set a boundary, when to say no, and when it's time to move on from a group.

I don't view any of my past relationships as bad; I see them all as good now because they taught me something and/or allowed me to take better care of myself.

★*TIP*: *Get perspectives from people you know and trust. Sometimes you can't see another way of thinking because you're too caught up in what is happening. A variety of perspectives can support you in moving onward and up that spiral of life.*

**It's over.** It's in the past and you can't change it. You do have control over what you do <u>right now</u>. Your **point of power to change is the present moment** (read Chapter 6 for more support). Accept as best as you can that it's happened and quit struggling against it. "I am not what happened to me, I am what I choose to become," Carl Jung wisely stated. Ruminating on something keeps you powerless and won't support you in moving forward. You can't change the past no matter how hard you try. (Trust me, I've tried!)

*Don't go down the "I've been wronged" rabbit hole.* I have to admit I've been sucked down this route more often than I care to admit and it's not fun. It might temporarily make you feel better, but for me it's like eating a donut. I feel really good for a while only to feel worse later. **Feeling wronged takes up a lot of energy.** Try and take things at face value and don't link the situation or person to your ego. And yes, this can be a real challenge. See if you can distance yourself and remain neutral about what happened. Can you gain a perspective that's not from your ego?

Some things that have helped me include saying to myself, "Well, I've cleared up some karma," "Thank goodness I've completed that lesson," and "I'm so grateful that person is out of my life."

Good questions to ask are:

> "What can I learn from this person or event?"
> "How did I contribute to what happened?"
> "What can I do differently in the future?"

By **bringing it back to me, I empower myself** to make better choices and move forward.

**①IMPORTANT NOTE:** *You may have faced a serious miscarriage of justice. If the option to seek closure is there, do what you need to do. Try not to spend your days and nights plotting revenge. I encourage you to concentrate much of your time and effort on how you can heal.*

*Don't play the victim.* When you **play the victim you remain stuck.** It can be really challenging to release your victim mentality. I was pretty darn good at playing the victim. It felt safe to be in a cocoon of "woe is me." One day my brother said to me, "You always see yourself as a victim." I was able to hear him and it was a giant wake-up call that started my journey to examine how and why I felt victimized. With that knowledge, I began healing.

As a friend Matt said to me when I was in a rage about a person who took advantage of me in a humongous way: "There's no court in the cosmos that will punish her and reward you." If you're up for it, model Lisa who was getting a divorce, by examining what role you played.

How can you get out of feeling and thinking like a victim? What benefit are you getting by feeling this way? What do you need to do to move past what happened? **Instead of focusing on "Why me?" or "Why did this happen?" ask yourself what you can do to heal and move forward.** How can you empower yourself? Seeking professional support, great self-care, and honest self-reflection are ways to release past hurts.

*Figure out what support and healing you need.* I believe many of us are taught that we have to figure it out on our own or that asking for help is a sign of weakness. I now believe that being vulnerable can be very empowering. Many times I'd struggle and suffer in silence and keep my pain a secret. As I shared my hurt with others and asked for support, it made a huge difference. I felt like a burden had been lifted and as I told my story a little bit of pain would leave each time.

What support do you need? Do you need to check in with your best friend daily? Would having meals delivered allow you much needed rest? How about a massage or pedicure to lift your spirits? Create a comfort list of what you need now that you can pull out when you need support.

It's also important to **have a team you can reach out to when you're struggling.** What family and friends can be there for you? When I was struggling, I had a friend check in with me each week to make sure I was getting out of bed and practicing self-care to support my well-being. If you don't have a strong support system, consider finding an online community or professional guidance.

*Reframe your focus.* Having gratitude can be one of the most powerful actions you can do. While you'll go through hard times, or might not get what you desire, you understand that you have so much to be grateful for in life.

**Where the attention goes the energy flows.** By focusing on gratitude, you support your healing process. If you don't have a regular daily gratitude practice, I highly recommend beginning one. Write down 5 things you're grateful for daily and try not to repeat anything for 14 days. Your list can include everything from, "I'm grateful for my friend Kaadi for editing this book," to "I'm appreciative of fuzzy socks for keeping my feet warm." Don't limit yourself on your gratitude lists.

*Find the golden nugget.* Look back at the farmer story. Can you see how what happened to you had some benefits? What good can you find from an event that did or didn't happen? I try and do this every time I'm challenged. It isn't always easy, especially if I've been through a tough time.

For over three years, I belonged to a women's group and the cruelty of one woman was the breaking point for me to leave. It was a conscious decision and when I made it, I felt a huge weight was lifted from me. Despite all the nastiness I went through, I sought out the golden nuggets. I wrote them down so I could pull them out when I felt angry about the experience or felt like I was a victim:

- Saved a lot of money.
- Had Sundays with my family.
- Watched all the Pittsburgh Steelers games.
- Made boundaries and stuck to them.
- Didn't become a mean girl.
- Gained knowledge that I can use.

What golden nuggets can you find from your experience?

*Take time to acknowledge and feel your pain; don't do the spiritual override.* What I mean by this is, feel your pain and <u>all</u> your feelings about the experience. Don't rise above it or think that you're "wrong" if you need to cry and shout. Many of us were taught to suppress our emotions or turn the other cheek. When you suppress your emotions in one area of your life, you end up suppressing your emotions in other areas as well. **You were hurt, so acknowledge it.** If you don't recognize your pain, it tends to come out, sometimes at the most inopportune times. I know that what others do and say is about them and how I respond is about me. It's okay to realize what someone does is about them <u>and</u> still feel hurt.

Those of us on a spiritual, religious, or mindfulness path can often get stuck here. You may think you should know how to go through this without being angry or hurt or do "better" because of the path you're on. Not true.

When you do the spiritual override, you aren't acknowledging the truth; you're distancing yourself from your feelings. I didn't want to acknowledge that the mean girls really hurt me. I wanted to rise above it. I've really been working on this because I do it more often than I realize. This response is more of a zoning out instead of a zoning in to the situation.

The truth was I didn't want to feel the pain or believe that I could survive the pain, although I know that on one level I can. Or maybe a part of me felt "You've done all this work, how can you still be so upset?"

By not doing the spiritual override, I can **be authentic, feel what I need to feel, and then push on** instead of staying stuck. Emotions are simply energy in motion and energy needs to move up and out or remain stagnant.

*Reassess.* What else can you be interested in if you didn't get the lead role in the play? Don't limit yourself. Sometimes you can't see the bigger picture. You might find a new passion. My dream was to be a screenwriter for the longest time. I almost sold a script when I was living in Los Angeles, but it never happened. Instead, I moved to Raleigh and turned my passion into supporting people in clearing clutter that grew into hosting a podcast, and writing these books. I'm also writing two personal books about my journey to support others in healing. I truly believe that my books will have a more personal impact on people than any of the scripts I wrote ever would.

You may have had no control over what happened, so **focus on what you can direct.** You can guide what you do, say, and think. You can control how you respond. You can choose whether or not you embrace good self-care or if you choose unhealthy habits. You can ask for help. Where will you focus your energy?

*Trust.* You never know what life will bring. Maybe you thought that you wanted to go to college in New England, but ended up in a college in the South and discovered a passion that became a career. Perhaps you leave a group, find a new tribe, and one of their members becomes your book agent. I can see in my life why some people, places, or events didn't work out, why my dreams changed, and when mean people actually helped me in the long run. Be open to what can happen and ask yourself, "What else is possible?"

*Be aware.* Awareness + Action = Change. I might sound like a broken record, but I think that this is so very important. So many times you're on autopilot and aren't proactive in creating the life you desire. If you always respond to a curve ball by drowning your sorrows by drinking, binging food, or going on a shopping spree, change isn't likely to happen.

Throughout this chapter I've given you suggestions to increase your awareness, including questions to ask yourself. Pat yourself on the back because reading this book and doing the work is increasing your self-awareness. Remind yourself of that when you want to quit or give up.

*Limit stress.* Don't try to tackle something new or add to your list. Get a babysitter and find quiet time. Enjoy a massage. Take time each day to find peace. Whatever works for you to limit your stress, do it!

*Be patient.* Depending on the situation, it may take time. Don't put yourself on a strict timetable. Even as you heal and move forward, there will be times where unpleasant feelings will surface out of the blue. Simply be with your emotions so they can be released. Be gentle and kind with yourself.

Some other suggestions to help you cope:

- Spend more time with family and pets.
- Develop new skills such as making decisions or saying no.
- Enlist and delegate help at home with chores, shopping, laundry, etc.
- Talk with a trusted friend, pastor, therapist, or coach.
- Begin or continue a mindfulness practice.
- Practice amazing self-care.

Remember, it's about learning to ride the waves and there will be some wipeouts along the way. Don't be afraid to continue to jump into the ocean of life.

Summary
You will get thrown curveballs. Focus on learning how to respond in ways that support you.

→ Take Actions:

- Concentrate on the present moment, not on the past event.
- Pick an area where you're struggling/feel wronged/hurt.
- Examine your perspective; ask people you trust for additional thoughts.
- Scream. Cry. Kick a pillow. Punch a cushion. Journal--whatever it takes.

- Get support, as you need it.
- Practice amazing self-care and limit stress.
- Seek the good in the not-so-good incident.
- Consciously choose to move forward.

# Chapter 9

## Do Something Differently

*Let go of the same old same old and try something new.*

Being an entrepreneur can be challenging. In addition to wearing many hats and having multiple projects, I have clients to serve. I felt this immense pressure to "funnel" consumers 24/7 because that's what the "experts" said I should do. When I first started my business, I'd attend a lot of networking events in order to find potential customers. I'm not particularly a fan of these events because I don't do well in crowds or with chitchat.

Despite my discomfort and lack of gaining new business, I'd regularly attend these events because it was what I was "supposed" to do. I'd usually leave discouraged, exhausted, and frustrated.

Finally, it dawned on me that I didn't have to go to these networking events to attract business. Instead of hurried one-on-ones trying to cram in a sales pitch, I'd devote time to getting to know someone and develop a real friendship. As people got to know and trust me, they'd naturally refer business to me.

In addition, I worked to find people I connected with online. It made sense as I work virtually and it benefited me because I really am a homebody. When I'm in my own space I believe that makes me a better professional. I also expanded ways I could find an audience, including my podcast and YouTube. Writing books was the logical next step and it's something I really enjoy.

If I had kept attending the same networking events and not become creative in ways to reach people, I might not have the client base and success I have today.

*Sally didn't have much of a social life. She became more and more frustrated and was spending a lot of energy not finding solutions. However, it wasn't from lack of trying. Sally purchased a bunch of books, listened to podcasts, and watched YouTube videos. She also asked for advice from family and tried to adopt all of the suggestions, but her social isolation only grew worse.*

*Luckily, Sally reached out to me. She wasn't incompetent or lacked the skills. What Sally needed was an outside eye to help her figure out how to be more social in ways that worked for her. We did some coaching and figured out the reasons for some of her challenges. Sally addressed her fear of being rejected, fatigue from not knowing what to say, and feeling awkward.*

*Sally and I brained stormed solutions that would work with her concerns. While she worked on her challenges, she also started to attend MeetUp. Sally loved cooking and was a foodie and in her comfort zone when she did these activities. She was genuinely interested in learning more and sharing her knowledge and it showed. Sally had fun and made a few friends. This gave her the courage to join a book club in her neighborhood, too. Sally continues to make new friends and feel less isolated.*

One of my assignments from a class I attended was to do each day differently for a month. Like taking an alternate route home from class, trying a new recipe, and changing my routines. I found using my brain to do tasks in a new way to be beneficial. I had to pay attention and focus more. If you're interested, Google how doing something you've never done before or doing something in another way can support your brain as it ages. There are some pretty interesting findings.

## Switch Up Your Routines

Many times you're unaware of what you're doing, feeling, seeing, or believing. You tend to **create clutter and remain stagnant when you do the same thing the same old ways.** You can still do routines, which can support you in clearing clutter, but you can shake them up and still get benefits.

Doing life another way can clear mental clutter because trying something new changes perspectives and the way you look at things. When you begin to see viewpoints differently, you notice more and this opens you up to new possibilities and opportunities. Switching up your habits can support you in breaking negative misconceptions you may have about yourself or others, and **bring you more into the present because you can't settle into autopilot.**

I used to have an online TV show where I interviewed guests. Putting myself out there in a very public way was a huge step for me because I always saw myself as a behind-the-camera type of person and exposing myself to possible criticism terrified me. I discovered I really enjoyed being front and center. This experience gave me the courage to start my podcast and open myself to an even wider audience. In the past, I would have been too afraid and embarrassed to put myself out there in that way, but because of building my self-confidence with other experiences, I was now willing to try something new. Worse case, I could quit. I'm happy to say it has ended up being very successful.

While I'm concentrating on mental clutter in this chapter, I wanted to share other ways that doing your day differently can help declutter other areas in your life. For instance, you can clear emotional clutter because you release fear. You go for it and get out of your box and comfort zone and discover that what you feared wasn't so scary after all. I used to be deathly afraid of public speaking. When I started my business, I could barely do a 30-second commercial about my business in front of people. I took a chance speaking in public and discovered not only am I pretty good at it, but I also really enjoy it. In addition, I now get paid to speak. Talk about a win win!

You can release relationship clutter by bringing excitement and joy into your life, whether you're single or part of a couple. You can get easily slip into ruts in a relationship (even in your connection with yourself), and trying different things gives you the opportunity to explore and have fun.

Physical clutter can be removed when exploring novel avenues because opening up to new experiences gives you energy and motivates you to let go of things. Clear your health clutter by experimenting with fresh routines, exercises, and healthy foods. When you aren't challenged, you tend to get bored and lose motivation.

Clutter is stuck, stagnant energy. **When you don't try new adventures you tend to become trapped in your comfort zone.** It's easy to become complacent and take the path of least resistance. You become resistant to change and equate familiarity with safety. When you do that you stay stuck and can't grow and learn. I bet we all know someone who is the exact same person we knew 20 years ago, who remains limited and hasn't enriched his or her life. You may look at that person and be grateful that it isn't you.

There are other benefits when you do life in a diverse way. Research has found that you can make your brain think time is going slowly by doing new ways. The day that I got married it felt like the day lasted forever--in the best possible way! I also find when I go to the beach that time slows down. It's my happy place and I don't visit as frequently as I like, so it feels new.

Experiencing **fresh ways of being also makes you feel good.** While it can be scary to shake up your routines, it can also be exhilarating and pleasurable. You're more alert and paying attention, and are living in the present moment.

Some say doing things differently can help with success. When I first started my business, I was the first eco organizer in the State of North Carolina. Some people predicted I would ruin my business trying to be green and organized. The opposite happened; I found my niche. People were interested in learning how to be eco-friendly when decluttering and organizing.

Shaking your routines up also reinvigorates neurotransmitters in your brain and muscles. Your body tends to feel better when trying novel things.

What can you do differently? What can you try? Have fun and make a game out of it. Here are some of my proposals:

*Take an alternate route.* Drive a different way to the, gym, grocery store, or work. If you regularly drive, try the train, carpool, Lyft, or bus.

*Strike up a conversation.* Talk with someone you normally wouldn't: someone who's a different race, religion, or has different political views. Be curious. Ask questions and then listen. Consider sharing something that you wouldn't normally share with a stranger.

*Use your non-dominant hand.* Explore for the day opposite eating, bathing, writing, brushing your teeth, etc.

*Take a course, read a book, listen to a podcast.* Check out something you've always been interested in, but never made the time for. Or try something that sounds totally not like you. I'd try welding after watching the show *Forged with Fire*. If you're already taking a class, sit in a new seat each class.

*Have an adventure bite.* This is what I tell my nieces and nephew when they're stalling at trying an unknown food. Explore a variety of restaurants or try an assortment of cuisines at home. Maybe if you were always afraid of spicy food, you'll discover you enjoy it.

*Expand your exercise routines.* Yoga or stretching? Walking around your block? Tai chi? A kickboxing class? Cross fit? Maybe your mindfulness practice has become stale and you can try something like mowing the lawn or listening to classical music to get in touch with your soul.

*Create.* What artistic endeavor can you pursue? Would you like to paint? Take photos? Throw pots? Write? Dance? Sing? What excites you when you think about doing it? Was there something that you loved to do as a child that you can revisit?

*Volunteer.* What are you passionate about that you can do to support others? Maybe you don't like people so much and an animal rescue or shelter would be a good fit. Or you love children and choose to work with disadvantaged kids. There are numerous ways to help. You can make calls, stuff envelopes, or raise awareness about a cause.

*Travel somewhere on your bucket list.* Maybe it's your hometown or a town/city in your state or going overseas. When is the last time you explored your own hometown? When my friend Kaadi came to visit I had a lot of fun exploring Raleigh with her and was delighted to visit places I hadn't been before.

*Learn a new language.* I've always wanted to really learn Italian and it's on my bucket list. If you don't have a local language class, check out an app like Duo or a class like Rosetta Stone.

*Explore Meetup.* I know that the quality of Meetup

varies from city to city. There are all sorts of groups that focus on dining, cooking, spirituality, hiking, sports and sports teams, and many other interests. If you're new to a town this is a good way to meet people. Attending group events puts you in diverse situations meeting people almost every time you attend.

★*TIP: Check out http://www.dodifferentdaily.com for more inspiration.*

Summary
Doing life differently can break you out of your rut, support clearing your clutter, improve brain health, and be fun. Discover what changes you can make to your life and enjoy.

→Take Actions:

- Write down new adventures you'd like to try.
- Schedule time to sample novel experiences.
- Record what benefits you've received.
- Notice what clutter has cleared.
- Switch up your routines regularly.

# Chapter 10

## Unplugging

*When you're still you can hear your soul speak.*

When I first started my business there was always something to do (this hasn't changed!). If I allowed it, I'd work on my business 24/7. When I started dating my husband, I began to unplug more. I really wanted to create a lasting relationship and that motivation, finding love, was greater than being connected to my business all the time. This was what allowed me to scale back my time on social media.

Being unplugged is something I have to be diligent about, and I have to admit it takes a lot of discipline. My husband recently showed me a video about being connected all the time. I asked him if he thought I was addicted to social media. He paused and said, "Sometimes." That was all I needed to hear to take a break.[7] My husband and my family are my priorities and I don't want to jeopardize what matters most because I need to check how many likes I have on Instagram.

*Marge would spend hours commenting, liking, and sharing on Facebook. She had no idea the number of hours she was spending on social media. While Marge's friends would tease her about it ("Do you comment on EVERY post, Marge?!? ☺"), she wasn't really concerned until she was reprimanded at work for checking her personal social media accounts too frequently.*

*When we began working together, I asked Marge to monitor the hours she was spending on social media. She assured me it was only an hour or two a day. Marge was astonished to learn that she was actually spending over six hours every day. Embarrassed, she reluctantly shared her numbers with me. I told her to focus on the fact that she now had a realistic idea of how much time she was wasting and what she can do to improve the situation.*

*I asked Marge if she really felt connected to people on Facebook. After some reflection, she admitted most of her "friends" were surface connections, but it did make her feel less lonely. "It's depressing coming home to an empty apartment. That makes me feel so alone." We devised a plan to commit to local activities for Marge to meet people. She's also exploring adopting a cat or dog.*

*Next, we examined why Marge was checking Facebook at work. After some conversation, she made the connection that she would surf whenever she was worried about how her work would be reviewed. Looking at baby pictures and funny memes soothed her anxiety. Marge and I discussed other ways to not only reduce her stress but also ways she could calm herself. I encouraged her to talk to her boss. Marge learned her employer was thrilled with her work, but he just didn't share his praise. Marge and her boss are now working on better communication.*

*With these life changes, Marge is on Facebook a lot less. She still appreciates that she can stay in touch with people who don't live nearby, but now concentrates her time and efforts "in real life."*

## Unplugging

In an article in the New York Times[8], 46% of smartphone users say their devices are something <u>they could not live without</u>. I suspect that number will only grow.

A blog on PCMag.com found that the average American adult spent 5.9 hours daily with digital media and the numbers have steadily risen since 2008.[9] There are many more studies and websites that I'm sure will confirm this. If you're interested Google a bit and see how your numbers compare.

What's your poison? **What do you need to unplug from?** Video games? Social Media? Your cell phone? Computer? iPad or Tablet?

Unplugging can be a challenge, so I suggest beginning with one item. It can be what or where you waste the most time like surfing Facebook; a bad habit such as checking your phone during meals; or spending time with videos instead of having personal interactions.

If you're unsure, ask yourself some questions:

- Where do I spend or waste a lot of time?
- What do I need to limit my time doing?
- Do my family or friends complain I'm addicted to something?
- Have any of my habits cost me anything? I.e. I was late to work because I couldn't stop playing video games.

Unplugging can be hard, so why would you want to do it?

First of all, it reduces stress. You aren't meant to be going 24/7 and always answering a phone or reading status updates on Facebook. If you don't feel comfortable without your phone, you're adding to your stress whether you're conscious of it or not.

You'll **also feel better about yourself** if it's social media you're using less. Social media can have a negative effect if you're using Facebook to compare your accomplishments to others. Researchers found that heavy Facebook use may make certain people experience feelings of envy, which in turn could lead to depression. In a study by the University of Missouri, they found that if Facebook users experience envy of their Facebook friends, they're more likely to have feelings of depression.[10]

Last year I saw a video that followed a popular Intstagrammer. The video showed the time and effort she and her family spent to create the "perfect" shot to post. Their "life" can't be achieved without a team. Nothing was spontaneous and it was posed. If you're earning six figures from Instagram, I can understand the time and effort you might need to put into your content, although I'm not a fan of falsely portraying your life. Most of us, however, aren't earning a darn thing.

Watching this video on the Instagrammer also reinforced to me that a lot of social media is like reality T.V.—not real. If you need to spend a lot of time and money using professionals to take your photograph, how accurate is it?

I'd rather live my own life than spend time being impressed with something that's fake and photo shopped.

Many times you're **not living in the present moment** and being plugged in **serves as a way to distract you.** The present moment is your point of power to change and create the life you desire. Unplugging allows time for important self-reflection and recharging.

Going offline also enhances your relationships. You can spend quality, focused time with people instead of glancing at your messages every ten seconds. You can focus on who is right in front of you instead of what isn't.

Take the time to think about **what you'll gain from powering down.** Write down your thoughts about what can improve for you when you switch the dial to off. Some of the benefits I found were: more time for reading; engaging conversations with my husband and friends; less anxiety; and fewer feelings of frustration that I wasn't measuring up in life.

Begin by practicing unplugging for ten minutes a day; if you can do more, great, but start with ten minutes. This is manageable for most people. If you can't do ten minutes, start with five minutes or 300 seconds. What's important is that you begin!

Write it down on your to-do list or block out time on your calendar. If you don't pencil it in, or make an appointment to do something, it usually doesn't get done. Use a timer to help keep you on track if you desire.

★*TIP*: *Investigate http://nationaldayofunplugging.com for more suggestions.*

If you feel the urge to grab your device or surf the Internet, take a deep breath and ask yourself some questions:

- Are you afraid you'll miss something?
- Is your habit fulfilling a need?
- What are you distracting yourself from? Pain? Anger? Sadness?

Learning what's really going on with your need to stay connected can be very valuable. You can't change anything if you don't discover the root cause. Be honest with yourself and solicit feedback from those closest to you. Seek the support of a professional if it will help you discover why you're unable to let go.

My new favorite term is **JOMO: Joy of Missing Out**. So many people are stuck in FOMO (Fear of Missing Out.) I love seeing the FOMO acronym turned on its head. I can't tell you how many times I watch people taking video or pictures of their experiences without being fully present in the joy of the event or enjoying with others around them. True happiness is watching a whale spring to the surface; trying to get the best possible shot to impress friends or get more "likes" is not.

Be gentle with yourself. These are engrained habits for most of us. The good news is if you increase your awareness—which is the first step—then it will get easier with time.

Create a list of what you can do when you go offline and the benefits you'll gain. Better relationships? More time for solitude? Saving money because you won't be purchasing the latest and greatest? Keep the list where you can see it to remind and inspire you each day.

Going forward, can you continue to carve out 10 minutes a day unplugged? Is there a better habit you can replace it with such as deep breathing, reading, or meditation? Taking a walk or stretching? Pursuing a creative interest?

Consider journaling about your life before and again after you unplug. A few months down the road, compare notes. **How has your life changed?** Are you less stressed? Are you pursuing more of your passions? Have your relationships improved? You may be surprised with the results.

Summary
Unplugging does a body, mind, and soul good. Commit to making in real life part of your every daily life.

→ Take Actions:
- Pick one item: Facebook, cell phone, video games, etc. that you won't use.
- Commit to unplugging ten minutes a day.
- Create a list of all the positives you'll gain when you take a break.
- Practice self-reflection.
- Record what you learn about yourself, including why you're challenged to unplug.
- Find healthy habits to fill your time.
- Examine your life before and after unplugging.

# CHECKING IN

You're half way through the book. How are you doing? Are you staying hydrated? Eating well and exercising? Being more aware and mindful? Wearing sunscreen? Seeking support, as you need it? Stopping when necessary? Honoring all your thoughts and feelings? How well are you taking care of yourself?

**Are you making YOU a priority?**

Maybe you flipped through and only worked on two or three chapters. Acknowledge and recognize the work you've accomplished. If you feel like you need some additional support, check out my podcast *Clear Your Clutter Inside & Out* for more guidance and motivation.

It's okay if you need to take a break and come back to the book. It's not going anywhere and will be here when you're ready.

**Continue to pace yourself and make self-care a priority. You've got this!**

# EMOTIONAL

Emotional clutter can affect your relationships (screaming at someone for not getting your order right), your mental health (speaking unkindly and harshly to yourself), and your physical space (not being able to release objects that have a sentimental attachment).

Research has found that the people you spend the most time with directly influence your lifestyle. If you hang out with overweight people, you'll likely become fat.[11] If you surround yourself with people who complain all the time, you'll start moaning and groaning.

What's your emotional clutter? Are you jealous all the time? Bringing unresolved issues into your current relationships? Do you honor your emotions or do you ignore or block them?

What else may be causing you emotional clutter that you haven't considered? As you clear your emotional clutter, be aware. Are you more kind to others because you're more kind to yourself, reducing your spiritual clutter? Can you release more physical clutter because you aren't attached emotionally to your possessions? Is it easier to gain mental clarity because your emotions aren't running the show?

# Unresolved emotions clutter your heart, mind & soul.

# Chapter 11

## Better Be Good to Me

*You can't drink from an empty cup.*

*Self-care allows you to take your power back.*

I consider myself to be a holistic life organizer meaning I view everything and all elements of life as connected. When working with a client, I may assign homework such as "Journal this week," "Get a massage," or "Meditate." Self-care is extremely important and most of us don't do enough of it. Do you put everyone else first and take care of yourself last? This is the only chapter in the book that has two quotes at the beginning because I felt they were both profound and necessary to share.

*Megan had a lot of physical clutter in her life. She was overwhelmed daily and could barely look at all she owned. Megan's mother-in-law didn't help the situation with lingering stares at the mess and "tsk tsk's." Megan's short-term solution was to shut the door and throw a blanket over it all. However, when she did that it only increased her feelings of being a bad mother and wife because she couldn't keep a tidy house. Megan would stuff down her feelings of shame, embarrassment, and anger by eating a pint of ice cream or scarfing down a bag of chips. She had gained 30 pounds in two years and was trapped in a vicious cycle that started with her physical clutter.*

*Megan was married, had children, plus a small business making greeting cards. She was also the first to volunteer, always said yes, and would make room for others needs in her jam-packed schedule regularly. As a result, Megan was overextended and exhausted. She didn't have the time to pick up and stay organized. Gaining weight and not exercising regularly contributed to Megan's lack of energy to declutter.*

*One of the first self-care strategies we worked on was saying no. Megan began by saying no to something she didn't want to do or didn't have time to accomplish. Megan started out slowly as this was challenging for her. She committed to saying no once a week. The more Megan exercised her "saying no" muscle the easier it became for her.*

*I also had Megan ask for help. She needed the support of her family if she was going to get out from under all the physical clutter. Megan asked her husband do the grocery shopping and pay the bills and had her children do age-appropriate chores. She also asked her mother-in-law for support, explaining she needed assistance more than criticism. Megan's mother-in-law was happy to spend time with her grandchildren and loved tidying while she was there. Having her straightening and doing light cleaning was one less to-do Megan had to worry about.*

*As she got her schedule under control and received more help, Megan started taking time for herself. She exercised regularly and began to lose weight. This increased Megan's confidence and led to more balance in her life. Megan and her husband fought less as she had more energy and time to devote to their relationship. She kept allowing her family to help and continued her self-care routine. Having time to read, meditate, and get a massage made Megan more relaxed and content. She was less stressed and more content, which in turn, made everyone else in her family happier as well. As the sign in my mother's kitchen says, "If mama ain't happy, no one is happy." (My sign is Happy Wife, Happy Life!)*

## Spectacular Self-Care

How well do you take care of yourself? Are you the first one to always support someone else and the last person to help yourself? Do you continue to have toxic elements in your life or struggle to release bad habits? Are you challenged when it comes to paying attention to yourself and tuning in to what you truly need?

Self-care is so important and I believe **a huge part of self-love**. If you love yourself, you take care of yourself. Many of us didn't have nurturing or self-care growing up or modeled to us as children. Don't beat yourself up or be embarrassed. When you know better you do better, Maya Angelou said.

If you're new to self-care, it may be a challenge. Be patient and loving--another way to slip in caring for yourself. It's never too late to learn how to love and pay better attention to yourself.

There are many ways to be more gentle and loving towards yourself, so don't try to do it all at once. Pick an area where you're struggling or motivated to pamper yourself. If you're still unsure, is there a trusted person you could ask that can give you constructive feedback? One of the greatest gifts I have is friends who are honest with me in a non-judgmental way.

★*TIP: Schedule and block out time for self-care in your calendar. As you plan each week be sure to add time to nurture yourself so that it becomes a regular part of your*

138

*week. Reinforce your commitment by making it a part of your routine.*

I'd like to share this thought that has served me well: self-care isn't on my to do list because I don't want it to feel like a "to-do." I have two big white erase boards that hang in my office. I have specific breathing exercises and I mark a "B" down so I remember to do them. When self-care begins to feel like a chore or a "have to", it defeats the purpose.

I suggest being **mindful about balance**. You won't be able to honor all areas all the time. Don't put more pressure on yourself to achieve equilibrium. I'd encourage you to look at your life overall to see how well you take care of yourself. Are you eating mainly healthy and exercising most of the time? Do you take breaks just to be or sit in meditation a fair amount? Are the people who are closest to you loving and supportive? If your self-care bases are covered most of the time, you're in good shape.

Moderation is also important. If you're compulsive in one sphere, other areas may suffer, as obsessing with anything isn't good self-care. **Moderation is key**. Remember, life is fluid and not static, so some weeks you may get five or six days of kick butt exercise accomplished and other weeks you're doing well when you can get in one day.

Self-care means different things to each person and there's no right way to do it. Here are some areas to look for improving how you love yourself. This is by no means a complete or final list; there are numerous ways to show yourself kindness. What else can you add to this list?

*Health.* Do you eat healthy foods more often or consume junk food? Are you strict and very structured with your eating or are you able to enjoy food? Do you eat mindfully or rush through each meal? If you're afraid a cookie or a soda is going to ruin you, that's not healthy.

I had a friend Andrea who was very rigid about what she ate. I can respect that, but she took it to such an extreme level that I no longer wanted to hang out with her. We were limited where we could go out to eat and she'd refuse to eat food I prepared if it wasn't organic. Andrea would scrutinize every ingredient I cooked with and it was exhausting being around her.

How well do you sleep? **Sleep is essential to good health.** Getting eight hours really makes a difference not only in how you feel the next day, but also in how your brain functions. How many hours of sleep do you get each night? Are you able to take a nap if necessary? If you experience insomnia, can you figure out what is keeping you up at night?

How about exercising? Do you exercise regularly? If it seems like a chore, can you do something different that will get you motivated? I fake jump rope as part of my routine at random times during the day. It isn't a full time work out, but it's a nice break from the computer. I've also added an adjustable desk so I can stand at my computer instead of sitting all day.

*Nature.* I love to hike and walk most weeks. When I can't hike, I get outside and walk our cat Antonio and spend time with our cats in our fenced-in yard.

When I first moved to Raleigh and was house hunting, my realtor said to me, "You reject every house that doesn't have trees." I wasn't even aware of it, but it didn't surprise me. A place that has been clear-cut just doesn't feel good to me. When I'm sad, I hug a tree. Nature calms me and helps me find peace and balance in my life. We recently downsized and back up to a protected wetland. Everyday I see butterflies and dragonflies. Most of my problems seem to dissolve and being in nature brings me present to fully soak in life.

**Nature can really soothe our souls.** I encourage you to do some research about how getting outside can support you. Tree, or forest, bathing is something people do. Once you're in a natural environment, slow down and immerse all of your senses in your surroundings. Sit and relax or walk slowly through the area and really feel the sun and the shade, smell the scents that surround you, and listen to sounds that don't exist in most urban settings. Find a park, a pond, or a mountain to relax, reconnect, and unwind.

*Mindfulness.* Learn to meditate or do a mindfulness practice that feels good and that you'll commit to regularly. It doesn't have to be sitting on a zafu saying "Ommmmmm." **Simply taking the time to be fully in the moment in whatever you're doing is mindfulness.** Perhaps Tai chi or yoga, where you're doing both physical and mental exercises at the same time, may be more your speed.

Believe that everything is always working out for you! You get to choose in every moment. Having a daily gratitude practice is an easy, powerful, and simple practice. Perhaps you say what you are thankful for at the end of the day, while you're in the shower, or stuck in traffic.

*Relationships.* How are your closest relationships? Does your inner circle support you or share with you how it can't be done? Are you able to say no to people when something doesn't fit your schedule or just doesn't feel right to you? **Do you have healthy boundaries with give and take?**

You often become like those who you hang out with the most. Who is influencing you? Is there anyone toxic that it might be time to release? Relationships are like a garden; they need tending to and regular weeding.

*Body.* Do you pamper yourself? This doesn't have to mean a fancy expensive spa. Just taking a bath with scented oil can feel luxurious. Having someone brush my hair feels heavenly. I love Ulta and will treat myself to beauty kits and have fun and experiment.

How are you when you put lotion on your body or face? Is a ritual that you're mindful of or do you slap it on without a thought? **You can find a rich experience in anything you do.**

*Spirit.* What moves you? Are you doing what you love? What's your life purpose? Do you have a religious or spiritual practice? Being loving, kind, and thoughtful is a way to connect to your soul and others.

I have stopped listening to mainstream media and network news because it doesn't add anything to my life and focuses mainly on the bad. It just adds more stress and negatively affects my outlook on life. Check out something like GNN—Good News Network. I'm on social media and trust me, if there's something I need to know, I'll see it. I feel we're fed a lot of garbage and what a select few want the masses to know. Get outside your perspective and check out a news source from overseas if you still need to be connected to what is happening.

Another step I've taken to stay connected to my spirit is to create an alter. I've placed crystals, singing bowls, and prayer beads in an area in our guest room. This is a sacred space for me where I can meditate, dream, or simply be. This reminds me to **stay connected to my soul and focus on what matters.**

*Fun.* I struggle with this one because my definition of fun seems to be so different from many people. I rarely drink and am not a big partier. I love to play cards and games. What makes you laugh? I was out at a party and played Cards Against Humanity for the first time. I hadn't laughed that hard in ages.

I also consider hiking, reading a good book, cooking, and having an awesome conversation entertaining. Come up with what *you* consider enjoyable and don't be bound by anyone else's definition. And get more fun into your life!

Finally, **simply be in joy.** I was doing an online group and the moderator talked about people who don't let what others say or do bother them. Have the glass of wine or slice of cake, take a vacation or take time for a hobby you love, and don't worry about what others think, or feel the "guilt" that you're doing something "wrong". Try and find joy each and everyday. I've discovered that when I try and find joy, it manifests every time. Having Coraccio family naptime with our cats always puts a smile on my face.

Are you aware of any unhealthy or destructive habits that can be thwarting your self-care? Do you shop for what you actually need or to fill a void? Are you eating or drinking too much, not talking to yourself kindly, or running ragged? Go through the areas I listed above and see if there's anything where you can improve, add, or delete from your life to take better care of yourself.

## The Holidays

You can really let self-care slide during this time. **Do you know how to take care of yourself when the season gets stressful?** Are you able to keep calm when someone pushes your buttons? How can you make sure you're doing what brings you pleasure?

I love my mother but she used to ask me all the time if I was dating or had a boyfriend. I didn't get married until I was 44! Having my mom ask if I was dating or interested in anyone was really stressful for me and I'd hear about it every Christmas. With a younger brother married, it just made it more obvious I was single and made me feel alone. I had to develop a plan for dealing with this subject. My younger brother has the gift of making people laugh and diffusing a tense situation. I asked him to play defense and also checked in regularly with my close friend. After a few years of this, my mom stopped asking about my love life.

The holidays not only can trigger a lot of emotions but they can also bring out some of your spiritual challenges.

This is a great time to do some self-examination and make some healthy changes.

First, focus on the positive. Where the attention goes the energy flows. Keep your **focus on being optimistic.** My mom loves and cares about me and that's why she always asked if I was dating anyone. It's not because she thought I was a loser and would never find anyone. Concentrate on what you're choosing to create, not what drives you crazy.

Second, know yourself. **Understand your triggers.** When you realize what causes you to react, have a solution. If friends get everything they want for Christmas or Chanukah and over share, stay away from social media. If being healthy is important to you, bring healthy snacks instead of being tempted at parties.

Also be cognizant of how you usually respond and **make the choice to respond differently.** What others do and say is about them, how you respond is about you. If anger is your MO, how can you respond from love? Can you make a joke instead? When my mom would ask about a boyfriend, my younger brother would sometimes have a snappy response that we could all laugh at and diffuse my anger. I'd remind myself that my mom loved me and be with that feeling.

Remember to **be gentle with yourself** and don't beat yourself up. Focus on progress, not perfection. It's wasted energy when you try to be perfect because it's never going to happen. If you fall down, get back up.

Finally, take action. Awareness + Action = Change. You might be tired of reading this, but I see many people letting days, months, and years slip by wondering why their lives haven't changed and they're unhappy. Having a plan in place makes a huge difference, especially if you're like me and get overwhelmed easily. When you're caught up in the moment it's hard to think clearly and not have a knee jerk reaction. Or, as my Uncle Jim who is a practicing Buddhist suggested, have a response rather than a reaction. He's found that the added two seconds of reflection can make a world of difference.

If you **make a well thought out strategy**, you stand a better chance of being able to execute it. If your grandmother's going to feed you like she's trying to stuff a turkey, who can you text to let out frustration? Can you excuse yourself and take a brisk walk? Commit to calmly inhaling ten deep breaths before responding?

Here are my tips for good self-care at any time:

- Schedule time for yourself.
- Practice mindfulness, eat well, stay hydrated, and stick to routines.
- Sit quietly, meditate, and take deep breaths.
- Close your eyes and simply be present.
- Remember what you love about _____ and let that fill your spirit.
- Treat your body with bubble baths, massages, yoga, etc.
- Rely on your support team.
- Exercise gratitude.
- Create a self-care strategy. Have it handy and review often.

- Breathe! When all else fails, breathe.

A friend on Facebook offered this sage advice, "What I used to long for from other people, I'm giving to myself." I love this. If you find yourself looking to others to fill a need, what can you do for yourself? Gift yourself what you need and desire.

Summary
Self-care is important and a significant part of self-love. Practice taking care of yourself, but don't make it another "to do", until it's a regular part of your routine. You deserve it.

### → Take Actions:

- Decide where you'd like to begin, or increase, your self-care.
- Commit to practicing daily acts of attention in the area/s you choose.
- Go on a news "fast": try not watching or listening to the news for a day.
- Schedule self-love appointments.
- Release, or work to improve, an unhealthy habit.
- Dream, feel, see, believe, and focus on what's important.
- Know your triggers: who, what, where, when, and why.
- Acknowledge what upsets you and don't judge it.
- Remember what's important and let the emotional clutter go.

# Chapter 12

## When Life Knocks You Down

*Expect the best, but prepare for the worst.*

When I was in college I'd heard through the grapevine that someone I knew, Callie, had been rejected by a sorority. Callie was so devastated and distraught that her mother and boyfriend had to drive hundreds of miles to console her. I was told when they arrived Callie was hysterically crying. Her mother always tried to shield Callie from disappointment because she didn't want to see her daughter hurt. Although her mother's actions came from a place of love, because Callie had never had any major upsets, setbacks, or challenges, she had a complete meltdown when she "lost". Her self-worth had been tied into being accepted by the sorority. The first time Callie didn't get what she really wanted, she couldn't cope.

You read a lot about helicopter parents these days and I've had friends share that more and more students become distraught over inconsequential events, such as not getting the class or grade they wanted. While not being picked for a sorority or fraternity can be disappointing, it shouldn't warrant complete devastation. If you know how to handle challenges or when life doesn't give you what you desire, it's a lot easier to handle heartache. The better prepared you are, the easier it is to cope.

*When I lived in Los Angeles, I had a friend, Sarah, who when she was rejected from a writing program, completely withdrew from life. For so many years, Sarah's focus, drive, and wishes were on being a part of this writing program. Sarah kept her nose to the grindstone and worked really hard. She was talented, but, ultimately, not the right fit for the program.*

*Sarah became very depressed. Getting out of bed each day was a challenge and it took all her energy to keep her job. Sarah shut out her friends and couldn't see any future that didn't involve being part of this writing program. Fortunately, Sarah had a good group of loved ones who cared for her and weren't going to allow her to succumb to being rejected. Her friends took turns checking in on Sarah and helping in any way they could.*

*When she was in a better space, Sarah's friends talked to her about creating new dreams for herself. Buoyed by her friends, Sarah began to write screenplays and even had a movie optioned. Although her script never became a movie, it showed Sarah she had other possibilities in life and didn't have to go the traditional route to get her material read. With the advantages of self-publishing, she is now working on a novel. While it wasn't the road she would have chosen, Sarah continued her love of writing while realizing what a great group of friends she has.*

There's currently a concern for the resiliency of children. If you teach kids good skills and model healthy behavior, it will serve them well in life. You can learn to ride the emotional waves of life instead of being overwhelmed and drowned.

## Planning for Emotional Health
If you have a coping strategy, when you're caught off guard, it can help you navigate your setbacks and upset.

You can see it as a blip on the screen of life and not fall into despair or depression.

Understand that there can be degrees of how much care you need and how you plan to cope with challenges. You'll most likely need more support if someone close to you dies and less assistance if you didn't receive a promotion at work. However, you are unique; respect that. Maybe not getting a promotion is a major event for you and I encourage you to seek as much help as necessary.

Here are my thoughts for riding the emotional waves of life.

*Be aware of what's going on and how you're feeling.* Looking back in my life, I realize there were times when I was depressed. I didn't have enough knowledge to understand depression, or people in my life, to see what was happening. If I don't know I have a problem, I can't fix it. If you suffered an upset, has your appetite changed recently? How about your sleep habits? How are you feeling in general: in joy and uplifted or sad and angry? If you know, for example, that you're not feeling well, this can prompt you to see a doctor.

**Pay attention** and put down your phone or get off social media so you can tune in to your feelings. Has your behavior changed? Have you lost enthusiasm for something you love? Are you more withdrawn or moody? If you notice something is wrong, find an expert who can help put you on the path to wellness.

*Allow your feelings to flow.* I suffered some trauma as a child and buried it. It wasn't until much later in life that I was able to face what had happened to me. I never understood why I would randomly feel anger or sadness or why it seemed to come at the most inopportune times. I now understood that it was relieving the pressure because I never allowed myself to own all the pain, sadness, and anger that I was feeling. Once I was able to acknowledge, release, and heal the traumatic event and emotions, I could truly move forward.

I encourage you to honor whatever feelings come up and let them express themselves however they show up. (I go into more detail about acknowledging your emotions in Chapter 15, *Feel Your Feelings.*)

*Listen to your thoughts.* Avoid any urge to judge, blame, lecture, or say what you think you should have done. Now is not the time to visit the wouldas, shouldas, couldas. What's most vital is getting through the moment of all your emotions. It's important for you to share how you're feeling and allow others to listen. Many times you need to tell the story a few times to release it; I know that it's true for me. Be patient with yourself and others, even if you're repeating the story for the tenth time.

*Find solutions.* I encourage you to come up with some solutions on your own. I always tell my clients they know what's best for them and it's my job to help them find their innate wisdom. Many times you're conditioned to suck it up or to feel hopeless and helpless as though you don't have any choices.

When you have a **clear picture of what happened, the time has come to contemplate what you want to do** to address the situation. Do you need closure? Take action? Set boundaries? Perhaps you seek additional support such as a therapist or spiritual advisor. Maybe you schedule time to address the other person(s) involved in the event so you can calmly express you're feelings and what you need going forward. You may find yourself making the decision to end your association with a person or group.

*Coping.* When I suffered a loss, I went off the rails and ate junk food for about four months. While this wasn't the best way to respond to my grief, there's a reason why they call it comfort food. You may need help in navigating how to best manage whatever you're going through. **Find healthy alternatives allowing you to express emotions.** If you're angry, can you release your anger by running, dancing, and hitting a boxing bag instead of lashing out at someone else? If you're sad, do you need to cry, listen to love songs, talk to your best friend, or sleep?

What do you need to do to deal with the situations at hand? Maybe you aren't in the frame of mind to clean, but ask friends if they can help for a week or two. If you're struggling with something major, such as the death of a parent, you many need to ask for more support for a longer period of time i.e. hiring someone to clean.

*Limit stress.* Now is not the time to worry about chores, obligations, or commitments. You need **extra love, care, and attention when you're dealing with major challenges.** It's okay if you let the dining room table accumulate clutter. You'll get to it later. Focus on the immediate problem and taking care of yourself.

★*TIP: Find a breathing technique that works for you. When you start to feel stress coming, stop and breathe. Many times you stop breathing when you're upset or stressed. Practice deep meditative breathing on a regular basis.*

*Be patient.* If you're going through a tough time, rally your troops. Surround yourself with people who will go to the mat for you. Ask them to be patient as it may take you a while to process and work through the situation. Be specific for what you need. Don't be shy. Most of us aren't mind readers and people are happy to help when they know what you need.

*Try and find the golden nugget.* One of the mantras that has supported me through life is finding the good in the bad. When I was single and really wanted to be in a relationship, I would list all the benefits of being single: I could sleep in, do as I pleased, and be make-up free. Write down the good you can find in your difficult situation.

If something is particularly challenging, I don't try to find the golden nugget right away, as I'm usually not in a frame of mind to do so. After the dust has settled, I take time to reflect upon the situation and find something. I was able to find gratitude for all the men I dated. This helped me be open to meeting my husband who wasn't the type of man I thought I'd marry. When reflecting on all my relationships that didn't work out, I now understand why and can't imagine being married to anyone else.

Finding the good in the most challenging situations serves you well in life. By focusing on being optimistic, it can help you get unstuck focusing on the past and unpleasant feelings.

*Life Happens.* Remember, experiencing disappointment, grief, misunderstandings, hurt feelings, sadness, anger, etc. are part of life. I like to believe that I'm a spiritual being living in a human body. As a human, I'm going to experience it all.

You can choose to be like the woman who didn't get into a sorority who felt her entire world fell apart or be someone who goes out, meets new friends, and finds other clubs to join. When life isn't turning out as you hoped, choose to trust that life is working out as it should.

<u>Summary</u>
Create a strategy for coping with unpleasant situations. Limit your stress, take care of yourself, and be patient. When you have clarity on the event, focus on problem solving and healing.

➔ <u>Take Actions:</u>

- Be aware how you can best support yourself in an emotional crisis.
- Define your support system.
- Consider sharing your plan with your support system.
- Commit to finding solutions that will allow you to heal.

- Limit stress and put anything non-essential on the backburner.
- Try to find the good in the bad.
- Ask for the support you need.

# Chapter 13

## What's Your Baggage?

*Are you carrying a backpack or a whole set of luggage?*

For over three years I interviewed people for an international internet TV show. While hosting my program, I longed to meet someone I could fall in love with and marry. While I was fulfilled professionally and in many areas of my life, I was lonely and ready to find someone with whom to share my life. As a single woman in my 40s, I'd often get questions of why I hadn't married, was I dating, would I like to be set up, etc. While hoping to meet someone, I had created a list of all the qualities I desired in a husband.

I was pretty impressed with my list. I only had one superficial quality—I wanted a tall husband.[12] While I would dutifully read my qualities each day to attract this amazing man into my life, I had neglected to create a list of what I had to offer someone, or areas where I could improve.

Luckily, for my show, I'd interview people from all over the world. I read books, did research, and knew my guest in order to ensure a quality show. Many times I'd share my own struggles with the person I was interviewing and I received supportive advice. Looking back, the show helped me clear my inner clutter and put me in the right space mentally and emotionally to meet my husband. My goal was to be the best version of me when we met.

During those three years on the show, I also did a lot of personal work. I had an a-ha moment one day that happiness came from within and I couldn't expect my future partner to make me happy. He could enhance my joy, but it wasn't fair, or realistic, to place the burden of my happiness on him. In my past relationships, I was expecting the other person to make me happy and would get angry and frustrated when he didn't. That was a big suitcase I was unpacking and able to release.

*Barbie was going through a bitter business settlement. Her co-owner, Madeline, left the business without any warning and completely blindsided her. Barbie had a range of emotions: abandonment, frustration, anger, fear, and sadness. She felt she couldn't get closure or resolve her feelings because Madeline wasn't offering her any explanations and wasn't willing to talk to her.*

*While she was going through the process of putting her business back together, I asked her, "How did you contribute to Madeline leaving?" Barbie bristled at my suggestion and was insulted. "What? She left me! I didn't do anything wrong!" I gently suggested that she take time to contemplate my question.*

*Two weeks later Barbie shared with me that she believed she carried the bigger load and she feared Madeline was dishonest. She had to admit that this was part of her baggage. "I was really angry when we last talked, but have thought a lot about what you asked. I'm embarrassed to share this, but I have a big fear of being cheated. My father had a business partner steal from him and we lost our family business. It was really tough for my family for a long time afterwards. I never wanted this to happen to me."*

*Barbie recognized that her baggage wasn't being able to fully trust and always to assume that Madeline was taking advantage of her. I had Barbie do some more work and she discovered this wasn't the first time something like this had happened. Barbie realized this was a pattern and felt that she was finally ready to break it.*

*Barbie knew if she didn't get to the root of her trust issues, she'd most likely have her next relationship have the same outcome. With my guidance, Barbie wrote a letter to her ex business partner acknowledging her role. To her surprise, Madeline agreed to meet privately with her. Madeline showed Barbie that she had never stolen from her, but her constant micromanaging, nagging, and accusatory statements were too much. Barbie had to admit that she ignored Madeline's request to hash out issues with a neutral third-party. While they didn't continue the business together, both Barbie and Madeline received closure and had knowledge how they can improve business relationships going forward.*

## What Are You Carrying Around?

What emotional baggage are you bringing into your relationships? Are you even aware of your actions and from where they started? Why do you do what you do?

Don't worry if you've never explored your emotional relationship clutter. **You can figure it out and make changes.** Review some unhealthy relationship behaviors below and see what rings true for you.

*Drama.* Do you constantly make a mountain out of a molehill? Are you always moving from crisis to crisis? Have you been told that you exaggerate a lot? You're

158

human, so you've probably been dramatic to some extent, but if it's front and center all the time, then you might need to check yourself.

Your **drama may manifest as anger, passive aggressiveness, or picking fights.** Contemplate how you respond on a regular basis when you're not happy in a relationship. Are you bringing drama and is it having a negative impact? Be brave and take a step back and see if your drama has created tension in your relationships.

*Criticism.* Is nothing ever good enough? Do you find yourself criticizing just about everything? Are people always bracing for your comments?

I moved this year and was invited on a walk with a neighbor. It had been a long time since I had spent time with someone who was highly critical of multiple people (including me!) in such a short time. This neighbor had shared she had difficulties with others in the area and I now understood why. No one likes being around someone who finds fault in everything and everyone.

You aren't always going to be positive, but you have to **be honest if you're negative most of the time** and if it's wearing down your loved ones.

*The Ex.* Do you constantly mention your former flames? Are photos and other mementos still around? How often do you talk about your past romances to your friends? Are you comparing your current partner to your ex?

I have to admit I was guilty of this and I had no clue. I had recently moved to North Carolina and was talking about my ex on dates. After a few dates, the guy called me out on it. Of course, he wasn't interested in dating me and it's easy to understand why. Maybe you didn't bring your previous relationship up at the beginning of a relationship, but is he or she showing up now?

Perhaps you don't compare your current beau and your ex out loud, but you're doing so silently in your head. How would it feel if your partner was always bringing up past people he dated? Would it make you want to get closer to her or look for the door?

*Distrust.* Do you trust your partner? If you experienced infidelity in the past does it affect your current relationship? Have you held back and not shared something with your partner?

If you **don't fully trust your partner it can manifest itself into being needy, clingy, snooping, and invading privacy.** Have you done any of these activities in your relationships?

I mentioned a client in a previous chapter who experienced infidelity. She had to examine how she contributed to it by always assuming he was cheating and voicing her lack of trust. If she doesn't course correct, she'll repeat the mistake.

*Tear down that wall.* Emotional intimacy is just as important as physical intimacy. To have a solid foundation and truly connect with your partner, **you** need to be able to share your inner most thoughts. Clearing any roadblocks helps release your emotional clutter.

Do you hold back your emotions? Are you reliving traumas from the past and feel you can't express yourself? What have you been holding back from sharing and why? This habit can be difficult to break, so you may need help learning how to connect.

*Commitment phobia.* You probably know someone who you joke about who is afraid of being in an exclusive relationship. You may be averse to committing because you haven't found the right person and you know that you'll commit when you find the best person for you. However, you may be unable to pledge your love to one person.

Ask yourself some probing questions. Do you really want to be single? What's keeping you from committing? What makes you hesitate? Is it the wrong person or are you afraid?

Don't get discouraged if you see yourself in any of these examples. You can change your behaviors.

★*TIP: Take this emotional intelligence quiz to learn a little bit more about yourself. It's free and you don't have to sign up: https://www.arealme.com/eq/en/*

## How Your Baggage Shows Up
Now that you can see what luggage you may be carrying, there are a few ways it may be showing up in your relationship. **Don't get discouraged if you see**

161

**yourself when reading these behaviors.** Honestly examine your behavior and see how you baggage is creating challenges in your relationships. Journaling is a great way to figure out how you may unknowingly sabotage yourself. What's most important is acknowledging what you're doing and taking steps to correct your behaviors.

I didn't meet my husband until later in life. While I wish we would have met earlier, I'm grateful that I had the time to work on myself so I that I could be the best possible me when I met him. Even if you'd really like to be in a relationship right now, it's worth the time and effort to do the inner work so that you can attract a healthy relationship. Even if you aren't looking for a romantic relationship, your baggage affects all your connections. Strong, healthy friendships can make a huge difference in your life.

*The Blame Game.* When I was in my twenties I got really angry with a guy I was dating. He was supposed to understand my feelings and respect them. I was sure our communication problems were not because of me. One night, exasperated, he said, "I can't read your mind!" Instead of continuing to fault him for our communication problems, I had to own my part.

Do you believe that the cause of your problems is always outside of yourself? Are you never at fault? Have you found yourself blaming your parents, your ex, friends, or the government for the difficulties you experience in life?

If you **feel like you're always a victim of life and nothing ever goes your way, you're stuck.** The first time you feel any emotional pain in a relationship you're likely to blame your partner.

*Control.* Wanting to orchestrate, control, and manage life often stems from a desire to feel safe. **Fear of not being in control may lead you to coerce, manipulate, smother, and micro-manage people.** You might get angry and stressed when people don't do as you desire. Relationships are often messy and unpredictable; if you can't handle that then you may not be ready for a healthy, mature relationship.

I have to admit I still struggle with this. When I find myself starting to control a situation or a person, I stop and take some deep breaths. I ask myself why I feel the need to control. Perhaps I feel unsafe or something is triggering a memory. Breathing helps me center and ward off a knee jerk reaction.

*Unable to receive criticism.* A relationship involves give and take as you find out each other's boundaries: what makes your partner happy, what he or she likes, and what drives him or her crazy. If you become defensive, angry, indignant, or sulky when criticized, then your partner will never be able to communicate his or her needs to you. He or she will constantly be tiptoeing around you and you won't be able to create a strong foundation for a healthy relationship.

Criticism is a part of life and **constructive criticism can be very valuable.** Someone who loves you is most likely going to be offering valuable feedback that can help you.

I'm very fortunate that my husband and close friends tell it to me straight. I always check in with my husband to see how I can be a better wife. At first, it was hard to hear that I was less than a perfect Unicorn, but I know that my husband loves me unconditionally. Because he's very loving in his delivery, I'm more open and less fearful of criticism.

*Non-Stop Negativity.* Do you moan, groan, and kvetch a lot? Do you focus on the negative in every situation and make sure everyone around is aware? Negative people are emotionally draining. If you're a mainly negative person, finding a new relationship won't suddenly make you optimistic. There's a good chance that you'll focus your criticism on the person you're dating.

Someone once said to me that I was negative. This really surprised me. He told me to read over my Facebook posts. I did and he was right. I wasn't aware how negatively I was coming across. It was a wake up call for me and put me on the path to being more positive. You can change how you respond.

Examine why you're negative. I found out that I did this as **an unhealthy way to get my needs met.** I falsely believed that I wasn't allowed to ask for what I desired and would complain when I didn't have what I wanted.

With this light bulb moment, I began to ask directly for what I needed.

*Living in the Past.* If you're stuck in the past you're unlikely to look towards the future or enjoy the present, which is your point of power to change and create what you desire. You can't change the past, but you can change your response to it and how much time you choose to spend reliving it.

2018 was the hardest year of my adult life. I remember I was spending way too much time on past hurts. I had to release the past and accept that I couldn't change it and trust that everything was unfolding for my highest good. Do I still have moments of upset? Yes, but the key is I don't stay there and spend time ruminating on "what could have been."

Pay attention to your thoughts. You may be surprised at how much time you're spending in the past (or future) and how you aren't really present. Review Chapter 7 *Past, Present, or Future* for more tips.

## How to Release Your Baggage
The first step in tackling any problem is to admit that you have one. Sometimes this is harder than you may realize. It isn't easy admitting you aren't perfect or far from it. I encourage you to view yourself as *perfectly imperfect*. Everyone has areas for improvement. This is the time to be your own best friend and not your own worst enemy.

*Pay attention.* What are the main themes in your relationships? What causes a strong reaction for you? What are some common themes in your conflicts in relationships? Feeling unheard? Abandonment? Jealousy? Criticism?

Are you present most of the time or find yourself drifting into the past or future? What do you argue about a lot? Do you freely express yourself?

*Martha had a huge fear of abandonment because as a child her father died and her mother was unable to give her the support she needed. She developed a fear of being left behind that carried over to her romantic relationships. As a result Martha was clingy and needy and this pushed away suitors. When she examined her behaviors, she began to course correct. Martha had the courage to tell her current boyfriend her fears and how she was working to release them. Martha asked him to support her through her process and he did.*

*Do some soul searching.* Once you figure out some common themes, note where else in your life you've felt this way: a job, past relationships, with your family, certain friends. When was the first time you remember feeling this way? Can you recall the details of the event? This can support you in figuring out the root cause. Journal about what you're discovering. What thoughts, beliefs, and behaviors weigh you down? Be honest and don't judge.

Can you identify the source of the thought/belief?

You may find that it was a **false belief that someone else planted in you.** When I was in junior high my art teacher thought I had zero artistic talent. I held on to that for years. I took an oil painting class in my late 20s and discovered I'm not half bad. Painting brings me peace and joy. When I went back to when I first thought I wasn't an artist, I was able to see that was someone else's opinion and not my own.

Where did you pick up your belief? Do you dread the holidays because your parents drank too much? Did you have a sibling who was the favorite and left you feeling invisible? Acknowledge the painful memories but don't get stuck in them. Many times when you fully own your emotions, you can release them.

*Don't play the victim.* Victim mentality keeps you stuck and unable to move forward. You probably know someone who sees him or herself as a victim. How happy do you think he or she really is? Do you like spending time with him or her? Is she or he interested in doing self-examination or just complaining?

If you're willing to look, you'll find the positives. I had a client who suffered from abuse as a child. Wendy realized one day that she's most grateful for her compassion and credits her abuse for giving her that strength.

You can change your perspective of the story from bad to good if you choose. Even better, you can release the story entirely and spend your time in the present moment.

*Acceptance.* The past can't be changed; make peace with every aspect. It isn't worth your time or energy to go down that rabbit hole. **No matter how many times you replay a situation on your head, it will never have a new ending.** Everyone has had struggles and challenges in life. People who are happy have learned how to move past them and concentrate on the life right in front of them.

This can be challenging, so I encourage you to figure out steps to clear this emotional clutter. My friend Amy would often ruminate on what she should have said and done. We figured out strategies for Amy to speak up for herself, create boundaries, and express her true feelings. The more often she did this, the easier it was to leave the past behind because she had no regrets and did everything in her power to create what she had desired.

*Create Sacred Training.* A mindfulness practice can support your general well being, keep you grounded and calm, and reduce your stress. **Find an activity you enjoy and that you'll do regularly.** Mowing the grass is very meditative for me, as is baking. I can get lost in the moment and it allows me to become centered. I do a mind dump during this time or reflect on what's going on in my life. I know if I don't do this regularly, I feel "off".

Remember, everyone has challenges; you're not alone! Be gentle and kind with yourself during the process. If you don't know what you're doing, you can't change it. Maya Angelou said, "When you know better you do better." Don't waste time beating yourself up. Put that energy into releasing your baggage.

ⓘ**IMPORTANT NOTE**: *I want to be clear that this chapter is <u>not</u> talking about abusive relationships. There's a difference between not being able to take criticism well and having a partner who belittles you constantly. If you're in an abusive relationship, please get help immediately.*

Summary

Be honest about what emotional baggage you're bringing into your relationships and how it shows up. Commit to being conscious in your relationships and being prepared to handle baggage when it surfaces.

→ Take Actions:

- Acknowledge your emotional clutter in your relationships.
- Practice self-examination to discover where your thoughts and behaviors originated.
- Decide what's your most important behavior to change.
- Discuss your findings with your partner if you feel ready.
- Commit to working on all of your behaviors that need improvement.
- Make peace with the past and find something positive in past hurts.
- Treat yourself kindly throughout the process.
- Focus on healing, not on "mistakes".

# Chapter 14

## The Green-Eyed Monster

*Jealousy is an opportunity to heal.*

Jealousy is all about you; it has nothing to do with the person who causes you to feel jealous. It's also an inside job to heal. No one else can make you feel less jealous and you can't ask others to not shine their light to make you feel more comfortable. The good news is you aren't alone in dancing with envy. I invite you to boogie with the green-eyed monster to own your feelings. The challenge is do you stay out all night, pout, and blame others for their success or use it to motivate you?

*Before I started my podcast, I hosted a weekly live international Internet TV show,* Reawaken Your Brilliance. *I was successful because I'd worked really hard and pushed myself to improve with every show. One woman, Shannon, who also hosted a show on the station, became jealous and badmouthed me. I heard from friends and business acquaintances that the only reason I was successful was because the producer had a crush on me.*

*Boy, did this make me mad. I was married, as was the producer, and it's not okay to throw around gossip like that. Not only did it anger me, but I also felt humiliated. Would people believe that my success was because of favoritism? Would I lose business because people thought I wasn't honorable? Al, my producer, told me that he admired how hard I worked and that I had outworked all the other show hosts. My numbers were higher than anyone else's as a result.*

Shannon also complained about me to other hosts on the station. I asked one woman about the rumors Shannon was spreading about me. The other host told me it was true. I'd shared that if we worked together we could improve the station and all grow our shows. Shannon suggested that I not be included as part of the team anymore. Whether or not it was intentional, I felt the other women distancing themselves from me and suspect that I was the subject of more than one unpleasant conversation.

It doesn't take a rocket scientist to conclude that Shannon was jealous of me. Perhaps it was because she had been the one to encourage me to create a show and I had passed her in both numbers and success. I confronted Shannon about her behavior with the hope that she'd take the opportunity to admit how she had tried to tarnish my reputation. If Shannon had said, "I'm sorry I was envious of you because I'd like to see your level of achievement," I would have understood and offered to share tips for success. Instead, she denied everything and continued to say unkind and untrue statements about me.

After contemplating what I was feeling and having expressed myself to people in the studio, I stopped doing the show. It wasn't worth the energy to stay and be around people who were unkind or distant. I also knew I'd like to do a show from home and not do it live. Although I appreciated Al immensely, I didn't want to be surrounded by petty women. I have found more success and a larger audience with my podcast that also led to this book. By being jealous of me, Shannon only harmed herself. She made herself look petty and mean spirited when she trivialized all I'd accomplished. Every single person who shared what she said about me told me they didn't believe her for one second. They said it was

171

*obvious she was jealous and she only made herself look unprofessional and envious.*

*Shannon could have admitted she was jealous, looked within to heal, and learned from her behavior. Instead, she chose to hold close the green-eyed monster.*

Has jealousy ever created emotional clutter for you in a relationship? Jealousy affects not only your relationship with others but also with yourself. Most likely when you're jealous, you're not happy.

Are you often resentful? Do you find people are constantly jealous of you? What are the habits of people who aren't envious?

## Why People Get Jealous

Keep in mind that you're not alone. Jealousy is a natural emotion that everyone experiences at one point or another. I was envious of someone who was getting married in Hawaii. Instead of sulking, I asked myself, "What can I do to feel less envious?" The answer was to plan a trip with my husband to Hawaii. Whether or not we get to Hawaii is not the point, it was about moving from jealousy to freedom.

**Envy becomes clutter because it masks what you're really feeling.** You can really be feeling possessiveness, insecurity, or shame. I once read that jealousy is often driven by self-critical thoughts. This was an a-ha moment for me. I believe we can boil everything down to feeling not good enough, not worthy enough, or not loved. If I were good enough, I'd be as successful as the other show hosts. If I were loved enough, my husband would know to take me to Hawaii on vacation. If I were worthy enough, I'd be making more money.

Other underlying causes of jealousy include:

*Perceived competition.* If you worked really hard for that promotion and someone else gets it, you may experience jealousy. As an entrepreneur, I have encountered this quite a bit. I left a local professional group because I felt an over-arching sense of unhealthy competition that rubbed against my business philosophy. When I first joined the group, I heard unkind comments about another person who was successful on a national level. I was shocked that someone who was serving on the board would share this with a new member. It didn't pass the smell test with me and I chalked it up to jealousy. When another person in the group received an award, snarky comments followed fueled by the green-eyed fiend. You may not be willing, or able, to admit your jealous, but others can see it clearly.

*Doubting your abilities.* If you are 100% sure that you have the same abilities as the person promoted, you wouldn't be jealous. However, if you doubt your skills, you may be fighting feelings of jealousy. Oftentimes, instead of creating a success plan for yourself, it's easier (and less scary) to badmouth and belittle.

*Needs.* Someone who needs money may feel jealous if you're financially successful. With easy access to social media, it's easy to see why you can quickly become envious. If you're lacking and surrounded by people sharing or flaunting what you need, it may be a challenge to overcome. It doesn't excuse jealousy, but perhaps you can understand the struggle to not be resentful.

*Insecurity and/or low self-esteem.* A person may be extremely self-confident in his or her career, but have low self-esteem when it comes to romantic relationships. I have to admit this was I when I was younger. I believed that everyone else received a dating manual at birth and I was left out. I was fairly successful in athletics, academics, and business most of my life, but hadn't much success in dating. I realized if I wanted to find a healthy relationship, I'd need to work on my self-worth. Being jealous of others in seemingly happy relationships wouldn't help find me love.

## Behind the Jealousy

Have you ever looked at the thoughts behind your envy? Take my friend whose wife had an affair. "What does she see in him?" would quickly morph into the downward spiral of "He's so much more Alpha Male/handsome/successful that me." Many times you can direct your anger at yourself because you feel not good enough, not worthy enough, or not loved.

You may internalize your negative experiences. If you felt ignored as a child, you may feel insecure. Or if you were never picked for a team, you may be afraid to venture into new activities.

Most of your **self-critical thoughts are on a continual background loop.** You aren't even aware that you're influenced by these messages. And self-care thoughts usually trigger shame. The amount of shame you feel directly influences the amount of envy and insecurity you have presently.

When you start to feel jealous, can you become present? Check in with yourself and ask is your jealousy about what's happening <u>right now</u> or is it coming from the tapes running through your head? Can you examine and see where the tapes are coming from and be willing to release this emotional clutter?

I once had a therapist tell me that I'd kept breaking open the wound and never allowed it to heal. That was a great metaphor for me and I really got it. That's what was happening underneath my jealousy. It really wasn't about what was happening in the present; it was old wounds that hadn't healed.

Have courage and face the situations in your life that bring up jealousy. "Everything that irritates us about others can lead us to an understanding of ourselves," psychologist Carl Jung stated. The more you can face the jealousy wildfire and put out the blaze, the more you can release your envious feelings. Realize that jealousy is overwhelmingly based on a false belief and understand what situations and thoughts trigger you.

## People Who Rarely Get Jealous

I want to be clear: you will get jealous, and it's not only about how you handle this emotional clutter but also the level and frequency you experience it. Review the list below and see what areas in your life you can strengthen. By putting these action plans into play you can not only lessen your jealousy but also give yourself an emotional boost in the process.

*High self-worth.* The hallmark trait of being secure

with yourself is being comfortable with yourself, loving who you are, and liking yourself. If you feel good about yourself, you're much less likely to be envious of another person's circumstances, finances, wardrobe, or relationships.

How well do you love yourself? Are you able to walk away from a relationship when you aren't treated well? Do you easily forgive yourself when you make a mistake?

Most of us can benefit from improved self-worth.

*Gratitude.* If you're grateful for all that you have in life, you're less focused on what others have and less likely to be jealous.

Practicing gratitude can be done in many ways. You can have a gratitude journal, state out loud what you're grateful for while taking a shower, say grace before a meal, or count your blessings before bed. If you connect an activity with being grateful, you have a good chance of doing it daily. For example, sharing three things you appreciate while driving to work.

★*TIP: Can you find a way to be grateful for someone who makes you jealous? What about their circumstances can you appreciate? Write it down and when you start to feel jealous, review what you appreciate about the person and situation. Does it change your perspective at all?*

*Unplug.* Researchers have found that heavy Facebook use may make certain people experience feelings of envy, which in turn can lead to depression.

While it can be fulfilling to connect with friends through apps, it can also become a negative tool because it's easy to compare what you don't have in life to what others have. Don't forget, people are only posting what they want you to see, and what they post is usually not the full story or sometimes even the real one.

Time away from the screen may be one of the best self-care steps you can do for your self-confidence.

*Celebrate others' successes.* Another person's success doesn't mean that you're failing. Even if you have similar circumstances, education, background, upbringings, etc. you are still on your own journey and path. You simply can't compare your life to others. Don't waste precious time or energy going down this unfulfilling spiral.

Desire <u>your</u> life. Compare yourself to where you were last year, five years, or ten years ago. I'm betting you'll have accomplished more than you think and have grown in many ways.

I believe what you put out you get back. If you cheer the wins of others, they in turn can support yours.

Do you believe Shannon would have had more success if she'd celebrated my achievements rather than try to tear me down? As I posted on Instagram the other day, "Confidence is not 'I'm better than she is'. Confidence is 'I'm great, so is she.'"

*Approving yourself.* I used to seek approval from others constantly. I couldn't make decisions unless I had checked in with someone first. I also used to worry about what others would think of what I was wearing. Now, I don't even think about it. My feeling is bring on the Birkenstocks! They are comfortable and make my feet happy even if I sometimes get disapproving glances from others. I am so grateful I'm not in that approval-seeking space anymore.

If you feel smug when others are jealous, you're insecure and your high won't last long. You're looking for approval outside of yourself when you need to look within. You have all the answers inside of you to change your life.

*Disregard labels.* This goes for your own categorizations as well as the labels of others as well. What you find fault with in someone you usually have within yourself. My coach Lisa would say to me often, "When you judge another, you judge yourself." When I find myself judging this mantra automatically pops into my head and I ask myself, "What's going on with me? What do I need to heal?"

You are more than your title or accomplishments. You're not your achievements, awards, job, salary, clothes, or relationships. That's coming from the ego. When I first left my Internet T.V. show I was a little lost because so much of my identity had been tied to that production. Without *Reawaken Your Brilliance* I wasn't a host, interviewer, researcher, and I wasn't sure how I fit in anymore.

## Handling Jealous People
I have to admit when Shannon was jealous of me I was uncomfortable. I often think, "How can anyone be

jealous of me?" This self-doubt of my talents created emotional clutter for me.

The more you shine your light, the more jealousy it attracts. You need to share your gifts with the world, so have a game plan to deal with people who are intimidated by your glow.

Here are just a few quick options of dealing with envious people in your life.

*Don't take it personally.* What others do and say is about them. How you respond is about you. I see countless posts on social media about people getting upset about something or someone. When I see this, often the hurt of the person shines through, not the "wrongness" of what someone else did or said.

Although sometimes this isn't easy, be like a duck letting water roll off your back. Try saying a little prayer or wish them well or send kind thoughts towards them and let it go.

*Ignore.* Sometimes this is all you can do and is the best course of action. Don't engage or respond and hope it dies down after a while. People typically go away or find someone else to attract their jealousy. Caveat: If you're in a work situation, you may need to speak to human resources, especially if the jealousy escalates and you feel unsafe. Trust yourself on how to proceed.

*Confront the person.* I'm not a fan of confrontation, but have grown more comfortable with it as I have aged. In the past, I mistakenly believed that confrontation was about fighting, but over time my beliefs have changed and matured. You can confront someone from a place of compassion and caring. That's how I chose to approach Shannon. I let her know that her behavior was unacceptable to me. I didn't yell or scream, but simply and calmly stated the facts as I knew them.

*Reduce interactions.* If you can't avoid the jealous person (if the person is a family member, for example), limit the time you spend with them.

*Be the better person.* I don't always subscribe to this choice. If a person is saying unkind and untrue things about you, it's perfectly reasonable to tell them that it isn't okay and it needs to stop. However, if it feels right, and you can do it without resentment, rise above.

What other strategies can you come up with to deal with envious people? After reading the suggestions above, which ones are you most likely to use? Consider writing out your thoughts and forming a game plan from there.

Summary
You'll experience jealousy; it's how you handle, the frequency, and the intensity of your response that's important. Heal the wounds from the past that are making you jealous in the present.

→ Take Actions:

- Examine an area or situation where you're jealous.
- Practice self-reflection: are you envious about the current situation or is it old pain?

- Find the wound where the jealousy might have originated.
- Release your hurt.
- Recognize and remove false beliefs.
- Take a deep breath when you feel envious.
- Incorporate habits to deal with jealous people.
- Congratulate someone on a success.
- Celebrate your achievements.

# Chapter 15

## Feel Your Feelings

*Feelings are simply emotions that are energy in motion
needing to move.*

Working on feeling my feelings has had a huge impact on my life. Since I was a teenager, I've been an emotional eater. As a young woman, I'd starve myself in an attempt to control my feelings. As I got older, I would binge eat when I was sad, frustrated, angry, scared, or disappointed. If it were an emotion, feeling, thought, or experience that I wasn't ready to face, food was my comfort. Instead of expressing my feelings, I'd stuff them and turn to food to soothe me. While I've improved greatly, acknowledging and communicating my sentiments continues to be one of my biggest life challenges. I've learned that when I honor and express my feelings, I don't need to scarf down a pint of Ben and Jerry's. As I face situations that stress me out or cause me emotional clutter such as anxiety, I don't automatically consume a bag of potato chips.

*Tiffany was married to Sam who wasn't comfortable with her expressing her feelings. Any time Tiffany would try to share that she was upset or angry, Sam would dismiss her. "I don't want to hear about it," he would grouse. When Sam responded this way, Tiffany would feel she was "wrong" for wanting to express her feelings and become depressed. Any time she needed to share what she was thinking, guilt now surfaced. Her shame and depression also added to her anxiety and many sleepless nights.*

When we began to work together, one of Tiffany's homework assignments was to express how and what she was feeling. Tiffany was to practice in front of the mirror, as it was harder to lie when looking directly into her own eyes. I also encouraged Tiffany to share her thoughts, sentiments, and struggles with around whom she felt safe. If Tiffany was feeling overwhelmed, it was okay to admit that. If she was feeling unheard when she was at her annual physical exam, Tiffany gave herself permission to speak up and share this with her doctor.

I also urged Tiffany to not judge what she was sensing but rather to view her emotions as guideposts to what needed to be changed in her life. Many women are afraid to express anger. Not only has society taught women that it's "wrong" to be angry but that it's also unladylike. Anger can serve as a great catalyst. If Susan B. Anthony and the suffragists hadn't been upset, women wouldn't have gained the right to vote.

Once Tiffany began to express her feelings, she felt that a weight had lifted. When she became more comfortable sharing her opinions with others, she shared her feelings again with Sam. When he started to dismiss her, Tiffany explained that she really needed him to listen and hear what she was saying. Sam repeatedly refused to do so.

After much reflection, Tiffany realized that it was important for her to freely express herself and if Sam wasn't open to listening, then she needed to end the marriage. While it wasn't easy for Tiffany, it was vital to her mental health. Moving forward Tiffany knows she needs someone who allows her to honor and express all of her emotions.

When you don't find a way to feel your feelings, your emotions will find a way to appear. Have you ever had a really angry reaction to something trivial? You most likely didn't have anger about the minor incident, but because you hadn't honored and expressed your anger, it surged at the "wrong" time. Unexpressed emotions, inappropriate responses, and denying your feelings create emotional clutter.

By honoring your sentiments you can see where you need to create boundaries and whom you let into your life. By following your emotional guidance, you learn to say no and have better self-care.

## Clearing Emotional Clutter

You may not be aware if you're suppressing your feelings. In many societies, people who express their emotions are viewed in a negative light. Many of us are taught it's rude or inappropriate to express how you really feel. Some people feel uncomfortable when people loudly wail and grieve at a funeral.

Do you avoid your feelings? Are you afraid to express your sentiments for fear of what others may say? Do you think you've moved past and dealt with an emotion around an event only for it to pop up unexpectedly and have it create relationship clutter?

With practice you can learn to express your feelings in a healthy manner.

## Avoiding the Spiritual Override

You may avoid some feelings because they simply don't feel good—grief, sadness, loneliness, heartbreak, and outrage are just a few. I've felt all of these and it's not fun. Other emotions that you sometimes create through the stories you tell yourself, such as guilt, shame, depression, fear, and emptiness, aren't great to hang out with either. Who wants to feel yucky feelings?

Research has shown that suppressing or avoiding your emotions can in fact make them stronger. If you're sad because you broke up with your boyfriend or girlfriend but want to avoid feeling sad and lonely, you may watch funny TV shows and movies or act as if the break up didn't happen.

I know that what others do and say is about them and how I respond is about me, and it's okay to understand that and still feel hurt.

If you're on a spiritual, religious, or mindfulness path you can often get stuck and not express your true emotions. You may think you should know or do better because of the path you're walking. Not true. It's important to honor your feelings and not judge them as being right or wrong.

**Emotions are simply energy in motion and energy needs to move up and out or it stays stuck.** You may be surprised at how much better you feel after you express yourself. Holding onto and suppressing your feelings is a weight you can do without. The other gift of sharing your emotions is that it allows others to learn they, too, can express what they're feeling. Goodbye, passive aggressive!

When you don't express your feelings, you aren't acknowledging the truth; you're distancing yourself from your emotions. I didn't want to acknowledge the mean girls really hurt me. I wanted to rise above it. What I needed to do was feel my anger at being treated poorly and then feel my sadness of feeling not good enough because some women were cruel to me. I expressed those feelings to two people I trusted.[13]

I've really been working on acknowledging all of my emotions because I hold in my feelings more often than I realize. It's more of a zoning out instead of a zoning in of what I'm experiencing. When I truly honor and feel my feelings, I can release them. Like all humans, I come from my wounds. If you clear and clean traumas and hurts then they don't keep resurfacing again and again creating emotional clutter. **Your feelings are coming up to be released and healed.**

The truth is I didn't want to feel and believed that I might not survive my pain, (although I know that I'm a lot tougher than I give myself credit for). Or maybe a part of it was that I felt "I've done all this work, how can I still be so upset about these things?" Remember, you are a spiritual being having a human experience, that's how.

By not doing the spiritual override, you can be authentic, feel what you need to feel, and then move forward instead of replaying emotions and wounds.

While it isn't fun to feel unpleasant feelings, this process helps you clear emotional clutter. You intuitively know if something is wrong, like cancer. Many people share that they knew something was off in their body, but chose to ignore the signals their body was sending them.

### Honoring Your Emotions

First, give yourself permission to feel. **You're allowed to experience whatever you need to emotionally.** Try not to judge an emotion as good or bad. Fear can be a good thing and serve as a wake up call. When you sense that there might be danger, you can course correct and leave an event, move away from a person, or take the necessary steps to not be a victim.

It's important to remember that **unpleasant feelings are a part of life.** You can't avoid feelings by trying to ignore them. "What you resists, persists," said Carl Jung. If you accept your feelings you can deal with them successfully and release them. What I mean by this is sitting with your sadness, anger, guilt, shame, etc. and really feeling the emotions. Experiencing the hurt, pain, and uncomfortableness of your feelings. While doing this can be unpleasant or difficult, please know that the pain won't last forever.

It's been my personal experience, and that of hundreds of people I've interviewed, that **it takes more energy and pain to hold on to uncomfortable feelings than fully experiencing the pain of releasing them.** It's never as bad or unpleasant as you believe it will be. All my guests said that it was harder to suppress feelings than it was to release them. When I ended a relationship I cried for about 20 minutes; howling, sounding like an animal, eventually exhausting myself. When I finished, I knew that my grief was over. That isn't to say that a tinge of sadness would pop up every now and then, but when I fully felt my heartache I was able to release it for once and for all. I have nothing but gratitude for the time we spent together. If I hadn't cleared my hurt emotions, I may have carried this baggage into my marriage.

When you feel your emotions, this may allow you to not act on your pain, such as hitting someone or abusing yourself. While that may not always be the case, you stand a better chance of not doing anything illegal or inappropriate if you are in tune with how you're feeling and release your emotions in a healthy way. Once you've released your feelings, you can channel that energy into something healthy such as writing, moving, creating, or dancing.

Also, when you don't express your anger or guilt, people can keep you oppressed and have power over you. If you don't direct your anger in a healthy manner, then your emotions can manifest as destructive behaviors.

## Releasing Your Emotional Clutter
I begin by lying down quietly and checking in with my body. I ask questions to see if anything needs to be expressed. Sometimes I get a response, sometimes I don't. If I don't feel or hear anything, I simply start to breathe. After some breathing, I usually notice what emotion in what part of my body is ready to be released.

I find breath work allows me to get in touch with my emotions. I have a variety of different techniques that I use. I practice breath and movement such as shaking my body while making sounds. I do this in our bed when I'm alone at home so I can be as loud as necessary. Emotions want to shift, so do what you can to allow the feelings to move. (If you don't feel or sense anything the first time you try, don't get discouraged. Keep practicing!)

I also like to get physical. I use boxing gloves to punch a square blocking pad that someone holds. I used to do this on a regular basis with my friend Stinky. He knew exactly what to say to really get me angry. I'm always exhausted when I'm done fighting. Maybe for you it's a spinning class that lets you tap into your anger. Bonus, you'll burn calories!

With dancing you can make sounds and move as well. Getting your thoughts out while you're walking may be more your speed. Make this a fun assignment and try out different ways to release your emotions.

★*TIP*: *Try screaming. You may be surprised at how much you've been holding back and how easily your emotions come out. Many times you exhaust yourself rather quickly and your emotions have shifted, moved, and released. No privacy? Lock yourself in the bathroom and yell into a pillow.*

There are many different ways that you can **become in touch with your feelings**. Set aside some time to test out a few practices. The more you do this, the easier it becomes. In the beginning, I could barely scream and now I'm able to max out my lungs. I've found with a regular practice, I don't get thrown off as easily when experiencing an unpleasant person or situation. Before, I'd turn my upset inward with unnecessary guilt or anger. Now, I practice deep breathing and let my feelings go up and out.

Once you do this repeatedly, you'll be more present with your feelings. Someone really upset me the other day. I slammed the phone and ran to the bathroom and screamed for five minutes. I released my frustration and didn't have to worry about the anger getting stuck or grabbing a pint of ice cream to soothe my self.

Feeling your feelings can be really intense so consider having a post session plan in place. Perhaps you do something lighthearted like watching a comedy or a relaxing activity like reading a book afterwards. Maybe order take out or have dinner ready in the refrigerator. I'm a fan of a good bubble bath.

ⓘ**IMPORTANT NOTE:** *You can avoid feelings for good reasons. For example, children who have been abused are usually very good at this. If you've avoided your feelings, beginning to feel your emotions may be very difficult for you. You can bring up some unburied trauma. Please, please, please take good care of yourself. Seek professional help, a trusted mentor, or a good friend to support you during this process.*

Summary

Feeling your feelings allows you to know if you're on the right path, alerts you to danger, enables you to create boundaries, and have better self-care. Give yourself permission to feel all of your emotions and express them in a healthy way.

→ **Take Actions:**

- Become aware of what sentiments you're avoiding.
- Journal to find any emotional patterns.
- Tune in and listen to your body.

- Breathe deeply to get in touch with your emotions.
- Try physical activities to release your energy: boxing, spinning, dancing, etc.
- Have a self-care strategy post "feeling your feelings".
- Practice releasing emotions on a regular basis.
- Be as present as you can with your feelings.
- Release any uncomfortable sentiments as soon as you're able.

# SPIRITUAL

Spiritual clutter includes not following your passion, comparing yourself to others, embracing a victim mentality, and/or not having gratitude.

This clutter can affect all areas of your life. When you go through life on autopilot, you can't change your life or have the life you desire. You can create stress and anxiety leading to mental clutter when you go against your values. When not following your passion you can get mired in sadness or depression.

What's your spiritual clutter? What else may be causing you spiritual clutter that you haven't considered?

Be aware as you release your spiritual clutter. Are you able to part with physical items because you're less focused on keeping up with the Jones'? Is your mind more focused because you're committed to your passion? Do you find yourself being able to express your emotions more easily?

# Spiritual clutter prevents you from reaching your full potential and sharing your gifts with the world.

# Chapter 16

## Do You

*You're unique; it's impossible to compare apples to oranges to bananas to grapes.*

I used to waste a lot of time comparing myself to others, especially with my physical appearance. I lived in Los Angeles for ten years and was constantly bombarded with images of how a woman was supposed to look. I remember the first week I moved to the City of Angels seeing a report on the <u>news</u> how to have a mini face-lift done during lunch. I'd just moved from Massachusetts and thought it was crazy that the news station would have a segment on cosmetic surgery.

After living in L.A. for a while and because I was insecure about my appearance, I easily got caught up in comparing myself to other women—how fat or thin; how attractive or not; the size of my body parts; how well put together my outfit was, etc. etc. etc.

Until I really appreciated and loved every inch of myself, including my flaws, I wasted a lot of time scrutinizing myself. I was miserable because the message I was telling myself over and over was "You aren't good enough!" I was exhausted from all the energy I was wasting because it had no end in sight. I was miserable, depressed, and frustrated. That's not a fun way to live life.

Although I still occasionally get caught up in comparing myself, for the most part I've learned to be in harmony with myself. This has made a significant difference in the quality of my life. I'm much happier, less stressed, and can devote time to being my most awesome self.

*Heather had just started her own business. She came to me because she was struggling. Heather had begun to doubt herself and wonder if she really was cut out to be her own boss. While she had a keen sense for her market, she was frazzled, overwhelmed, and stuck.*

*It soon became apparent one of Heather's biggest challenges was comparing herself to other entrepreneurs in her field. I told her that I understood how she can easily get sucked in to comparing how she's doing to others in similar businesses. I suggested to her that she wasn't being realistic as these merchants had been in business for years and she was just starting out. For most entrepreneurs, it takes time to build a business and Heather was hurting herself by having unrealistic expectations.*

*We spent time carving out a niche for Heather and her specific skill set. This gave her more confidence and reminded her that she truly couldn't compare her business because it really was unique. Heather also began to build alliances with other entrepreneurs so that she could give, and get, referrals when she wasn't a right fit for a potential client. She's now more focused, energized, and is building her business.*

It's been my experience that women (and very often men) compare themselves to one another all the time. With looks, career, money, parenting…you name it, women tend to be in constant comparison mode. What a waste of mental, emotional, and spiritual energy! I really hope women, and men, quit the comparison game. As you work on comparing less, I hope you'll pay it forward and encourage others to do so as well.

Comparing yourself to others can **create spiritual clutter by getting you sidetracked in spending time on what doesn't matter.** If you use your time to compare yourself to others, you won't spend anytime recognizing, cultivating, and celebrating *your* gifts. How will you be able to share your talents with the world if you can't appreciate them?

### Apples to Oranges to Bananas to Grapes

If you have low self-esteem, you're more likely to scrutinize yourself against others. You may compare yourself to someone whom you don't view as good as you to give yourself a temporary ego boost. This is a great example of what it's like when I eat a donut. That fried circle of yumminess is really delicious when I first eat it, but within the hour I don't feel well. Trying to make yourself feel better by stacking yourself against another won't do anything for you in the long haul.

If you size yourself up to others and this makes you feel bad about yourself, you can further harm your self-esteem. Comparing can also damage your relationships. If you're always concentrating on the faults of your significant other, how can you see all of the good in him or her? I know I wouldn't want to be subjected to hearing how there are much better wives than me.

It's human nature to want to see how you stack up against others. I also believe with all the advertising and messages you're bombarded with daily, it's hard not to let that lead you down the comparing path. However, **if you focus** on others, you don't take time to discover and enjoy your own path. You have your journey and lessons to learn. Even if you're weighing yourself against someone with similar circumstances, looks, skills, jobs, income, etc. you may very well have different paths and distinct reasons for having similar experiences.

Scrutinizing yourself against someone else is easy. It's a lot harder to engage in self-reflection. When you compare yourself to others, you rob yourself of happiness.

When you stop measuring yourself against others, **you'll see your gifts much more clearly and start putting them to use.** I desire to live in a world where everyone follows his or her joy and passion. Everyone benefits when that happens. What a boring world we'd live in if we were all the same.

Often your clutter represents something else—maybe it's to fill a need or to keep an emotion buried. When I wasted my energy comparing my looks, I was really attempting to control my depression. I was sad that I hadn't established a community yet in Los Angeles and was lonely. I've also found when I'm not able to be grateful that I'm really feeling disconnected from my source and it's time to reestablish my spiritual practice.

Can you examine why you may be comparing yourself? **What message is your spiritual clutter trying to tell you?** What are you blocking that you can release?

Like anything, changing a pattern takes practice, but by not likening yourself to others you'll free up energy that will give you the time and the freedom to improve your life.

### Putting the Kibosh on Comparing

When you find yourself comparing, stop. Take a deep breath. Spend time reflecting. Why do you feel the need to judge? What weaknesses can you improve? What about yourself would you like to celebrate? Begin to redirect your thoughts in the moments when you start down the comparison road. Take a deep breath and repeat, "Instead of comparing myself to _____, **I choose to focus on myself and how I can improve my life,**" or "What's the next step I need to take to move myself forward on my path?", or "How can I celebrate myself in this moment?"

I'm also a fan of combining a physical action to change a habit. I have a mala bead bracelet that I use to repeat a mantra. I touch a bead each time I repeat a phrase. Every time you find yourself comparing, you can ask, "What one good thing can I say about myself right now?" and touch a bead each time you share something you love about yourself.

*★TIP: Write down all the qualities you love about yourself such as physical attributes, personality traits, skills, talents, passions, and qualities. If you find yourself stuck, ask friends and family what they love and admire about you. Review this list when you find yourself seeing how you measure up to others.*

*Know your triggers.* There's no shame in admitting where you struggle and what can upset you. Knowing yourself allows you to be proactive and set a pattern for making healthier choices.

If seeing women in bikinis on Instagram makes you feel bad about your body and punish yourself with two hours of exercise, stay off Instagram. You can also unfollow the offenders and/or hash tags. If you get jealous of the elaborate party your co-worker throws and chronicles on Facebook or SnapChat, unfollow her for 30 days. If clothes shopping with friends makes you constantly compare waist size, skip the trip this year.

*Take social media for what it's worth.* Remember that social media is not always what it's cracked up to be. I saw one instance when a person photo shopped himself in front of a private plane. Numerous women, including celebrities, regularly alter their bodies in pictures they post publically. A lot of social media is about what people want you to see and isn't real life. I don't have the time, patience, and energy to create something or someone I'm not. I understand most of social media is a false comparison, so I don't let it wreck my day. Many times what people share on social media is unrealistic or fake. Would you be scared of a fake dinosaur? Then don't be concerned you aren't measuring up on social media.

I recommend taking breaks from social media regularly—give it a try—as it helps more than just your self-esteem. It enables you to spend time on what's really important for you, have more time with those you love in real life, and perhaps even save money by not purchasing something from the numerous ads that bombard you constantly.

*Release not good enough.* I believe all your spiritual clutter stems from feeling not good enough, not worthy enough, or not feeling loved. Know that you're perfect as the imperfect you. Eleanor Roosevelt said, "No one can make you feel inferior without your consent." Find ways to feel great about yourself and build your self-esteem. Some ways you can do that include:

- Say affirmations (I am loveable, I am talented, I am good enough, etc.).
- Recognize the difference you're making at work, with your creative projects, and to your loved ones (human and fur).
- Acknowledge all the awesome qualities you have.
- Exercise.
- Realize everyone makes mistakes.
- Focus on solutions to improve your life.

When you shore up your self-esteem, the actions of others are less likely to bother you.

*Material goods aren't all that.* The outside may look good, but who knows about the inside? As I age, the more I see how worldly possessions are less important. Having peace, loving myself, and being content are much more priceless than a designer handbag, title, and fancy car. Recalibrate how you measure success. How happy are you? How often are you at peace? Can you find joy in the little offerings in life? I know many people who are "successful" yet unhappy and rarely satisfied.

*Use as motivation.* Instead of weighing yourself against others to feel better (or worse) about yourself, how can you use it to motivate you? If you compare yourself to friends who constantly eat at fancy restaurants, can you learn how to cook? Would you be motivated to get a side gig like pet sitting to earn extra income to afford nice restaurants? If your friend just self-published on Amazon, can you block out 15 minutes to write everyday? Can you believe that because your friend accomplished his or her goal that you can too?

There is one instance in which I believe comparing yourself to others can be useful. If you compare yourself to someone who is less fortunate, it can remind you to be grateful. It can help you put your life in perspective and remind you of all you have to celebrate in your life.

Summary
Understand you're unique and really can't compare your life to anyone else's. Concentrate on boosting your self-esteem, taking stock of your inner world, and recognizing all that you've accomplished.

→ Take Actions:

- Notice where you're comparing yourself <u>right now</u>.
- Reflect on where you tend to review how you stack up (money, career, parenting, etc.).
- Journal about your experience comparing and why you measure yourself against others.
- Decide how to redirect your energy when you find you're measuring yourself against others.
- Create a plan to boost your self-esteem.
- Reframe other's success as a tool to motivate you or to be grateful.

# Chapter 17

## Give Thanks

*Gratitude releases clutter in all its forms.*

Each day in 2016, I posted a daily gratitude on my personal Facebook page. My friend Darla inspired me because she posted what she was grateful for daily in 2015. After reading Darla's posts on what she appreciated that day, I'd follow suit by saying out loud what I was thankful for in that moment. I found myself looking forward to what Darla shared because I was always in a better mood after reading her thoughts. Posting my own daily appreciations was a wonderful experience for me as it forced me every day to look for gratitude even when I believed I couldn't find anything.

When I was really unhappy, I barely had any gratitude despite having a rich life. I had my health, a home, business, family, and friends who cared about me. However, that wasn't enough as I was so focused on what I didn't have. I couldn't see all the bounty that was right before my eyes. I was making myself miserable by focusing on what was missing from my life. Instead of being excited for life, I was stumbling through it envious of what others had and complaining about what I lacked.

It also affected my business. When I focused on all the business I didn't have, while not acknowledging the amazing clients I did have, I attracted less work. My wake up call came when my friend and mentor Lisa called me out when I was complaining. Lisa literally grabbed me and walked me around my home pointing out everything I had to appreciate.

After Lisa's intervention, I began a daily gratitude practice. On days when I struggled, I'd remind myself of the basics that I had that so many others lacked around the globe: clean drinking water, access to health care, food, safety, and shelter.

I also began checking in with my customers about how they expressed their thanks (or not). Many times your initial challenges are only a symptom of something deeper. They serve as a call to explore your life more fully. Having gratitude is something I discuss with all my clients now. Simply getting into the habit of appreciating everything and anything can be life changing.

*Susan constantly complained about her life. She was really wealthy and her friends found it hard to listen to her gripe because she had numerous options that most people didn't. "Never enough" seemed to be Susan's rallying cry. After a while, some of her friends stopped hanging out with her and wouldn't return her calls. One friend exploded after one of Susan's particularly petulant rants, "You're exhausting to be around. You have more in your life than anyone I know and all you do is whine and complain. Until you can stop focusing on your perceived lack, I'm done with our friendship." This outburst from her friend led Susan to hire me.*

*Susan's inability to have gratitude stemmed from her deep loneliness. Her bitterness about being single manifested itself into kvetching and being annoyed at all she lacked in her life. We discussed how her grouchy nature was a turn off for people and how a potential suitor would most likely lose interest quickly.*

*While we began to work on a strategy for her loneliness, I also encouraged Susan to focus on what she was grateful for, but she was still struggling. I like to believe that the Universe/God decided to step in and help. A few days after our coaching session, Susan was at a park when a random stranger sat down next to her on a bench.*

*As they began to talk, Susan began to carp about all that was missing from her life. The stranger started laughing and Susan became angry. "What right do you have to judge me?" she demanded. The stranger told her that she, too, used to take much for granted. "I can't believe all the energy I wasted on what I thought was missing from my life. I found out this week that I have cancer so it all seems pretty insignificant now."*

*That conversation was Susan's turning point and she left the park with a new sense of appreciation. She realized how she had been taking her health, financial stability, and the people in her life who loved her, for granted. A side benefit to this new found gratitude was that Susan began to volunteer with an after school program for disadvantaged kids.*

I used to be a fairly negative person and I credit giving thanks daily for supporting me in making positive changes in my life. I understand that it can be challenging at times because you may be facing some real hardships and difficulties. Sometimes you're simply too unhappy to focus on what's going well in your life. The good news is that you can change and simply need a place to begin.

## Got Gratitude?

If it weren't part of your daily routine growing up, you likely never learned this habit.

Many people liked my Facebook posts, but not everyone. Some people were annoyed at seeing my appreciation every day and told me. I gently suggested that they examine what they were so upset about because it really wasn't about anything I'd written.

You live in a society that's constantly showing you all the material possessions you must have to be happy. Social media has only added fuel to the fire so you can see wild abundance 24/7. **Even if you're pretty content with what you have, you can easily find yourself complaining** when constantly bombarded with these images.

If you compare, you rob yourself of gratitude. You focus on what others have instead of the abundance in your own life. It can be so easy to take all you have for granted.

I've seen discussions in the news that some people are wired to not be appreciative. If you're truly someone who is born that way (and honestly I'm not convinced), you can make the choice to retrain your brain. You can learn new skills at any time in life; it's whether you choose to do so and will put in the time and effort.

## Having Gratitude

With gratitude it's hard to accumulate emotional and mental clutter because you can't hold two opposing thoughts at once. For example, you can't be angry and grateful at the same time. You can't have anxiety and be happy with what you have simultaneously. When you're grateful for all that you own, it lessens your need to obtain more possessions that can easily morph into physical clutter.

By having gratitude, **you raise your vibration and are more likely to attract what you desire.** Put this to the test. Spend a week complaining and focusing on what you lack in your life. How does the week go? Did you seem to get more of the same? Now try a week practicing gratitude. Did your life improve and were you able to see more of what you'd like to receive? Record what happens during these two weeks. Take note of all areas of your life: work, relationships, health, finances, and play. Did you release any physical clutter? How did your mental state compare in each week? What were your emotions in each week? Were you frustrated, angry, sad, or peaceful, happy, and joyful?

Do you share your gratitude? I love social media because you can really learn a lot about a person. Examine your posts, tweets, and comments. Are yours mainly positive, uplifting, and expressing thanks or are they mainly sour grapes, complaints, and negativity? You're often unconscious and unaware of what you're saying, believing, thinking, and doing.

Look at friends' posts that are generally upbeat. Do you believe they have a sense of gratitude? Observe your co-workers, friends, and family. Do you sense a pattern with people who are thankful for what they have? Watch people and posts that you're most drawn to following, hanging out with, and enjoying. Are they similar to you and what you share or are they different?

My maternal grandmother had Alzheimer's and my family was fortunate to have a caretaker, Tressie, who was a phenomenal human being. Not long after my grandmother died, Tressie and her husband, Paul, lost their house to a fire. My parents and I went to visit them around Christmas. Paul had been a minister. He asked if we could all pray together before we left. We held hands and Paul led us in prayer. He talked about how grateful he and Tressie were, for their bounty, and how they wanted our family to be as blessed. I started to softly cry because I was so moved by their ability to be thankful after having just lost everything and awed by how they could be so generous towards my family in their time of crisis. Paul and Tressie were people who mastered gratitude and chose to share this abundance with others. When you have gratitude you can see what truly matters.

Steven Covey said it takes 21 days to create a habit. Beginning today, **make a list of what you're grateful for. Keep it close** so when something comes to mind you can jot it down. Be sure to include the small elements—a pretty sunset, a delicious ice cream cone, or a smile from a stranger. My observation is often there's an expectation that what you're grateful for must be huge or what I refer to as the Oprah Winfrey "You get a car! You get a car! You get a car!" moment. Little pieces of life turn into the big enjoyments the more you practice gratitude.

★*TIP*: *Try doing your gratitude practice with a routine you already do daily. For example, say three things you're thankful for while taking a shower. Or write down five items you appreciate after checking email. Perhaps you share your gratitude for a minute during your daily walk.*

If you're in a challenging space right now, try and **have gratitude for basic necessities** such as having the ability to read, having access to health care or education, or having a place to bathe. Many of us have an easy pathway to goods and services that other people don't. And if you can't feel any gratitude at the moment, that's okay. Don't get discouraged as you can build your gratitude muscle. You're human, but I encourage you to make the effort. I believe acknowledging that in this moment you can't have gratitude is better than trying to fake it. When you're honest with how you're feeling, it takes the pressure off you to perform. You realize that you're not able to appreciate and your heart opens a bit more making it easier for genuine gratitude to slip in effortlessly.

Recently I was in a space where I wasn't feeling grateful because I was very hurt and upset about something in my life. The next day, I was shopping at a grocery store and saw a homeless man. I invited him to come inside with me and choose what he wanted to eat from the deli. He found a sandwich and I suggested adding a drink, side dish, and cookie. Everyone should enjoy a cookie now and then. Yes, he got a meal but that guy got the short end of the stick that day because I felt so wonderful doing something kind for him. He also reminded me that I'm lucky to have a home, food, and people who love me.

My gratitude was genuine and heartfelt in my experience with the homeless man. And it broke my block of not being able to find gratitude. Johann Wolfgang von

Goethe said, "At the moment of commitment, the entire universe conspires to assist you." If you're really trying to find your gratitude, the Universe/God will support you.

How often do you truly have gratitude for your food, not hurriedly mumbling through a blessing before your meal just so you can finally eat? Where in your life are you saying thanks just to get something in return or another perceived benefit, such as a friend's admiration?

I strive to be thankful for something every day. My life changed for the better when I incorporated a regular practice of being grateful. I was able to focus on what I had instead of what I didn't have. I feel more at peace, less stressed, and more joyful when I appreciate all that I have in my life.

## Loving What Is
It isn't so easy to love life as it is, especially when you might be having a tough time or experiencing real heartbreak. It's challenging to love your life if your house burns down or your child is sick.

Can you try to take your gratitude a step deeper and **love everything in your life as it is right now**? When you love everything <u>as is</u> you're already in gratitude. It's easy to appreciate everything when life is going your way but how about when it isn't?

I see amazing gratitude from people who have faced tragedy again and again. I watched stories from the Camp Fire in California in November 2018 as people shared all that they were thankful for although many lost everything. They were able to focus on the blessings they had right after a tragedy.

A better word, if you're struggling, might be to accept what is and work towards loving it. I was really sick recently and spent ten days in bed. I could more easily accept it before loving it. I was able to love it by saying, "Obviously I needed a rest and this was the only way it was going to happen. When was the last time I got to spend my days in pajamas? When have I been able to sleep and read this much?" By accepting what was happening, I was more easily able to move into loving what was my situation.

Oklahoma Thunder assistant basketball coach Monty Williams gave an amazing speech after an errant driver on the wrong side of the road killed his wife.[14] He's a Christian and loved that his wife was in heaven. Williams said it wasn't easy and he was heartbroken, but he was able to love what had happened to her. How many of us could find gratitude in such a terrible situation?

At the end of his speech, Williams talked about how he bore no ill will towards the family of the driver and the driver's family needed prayers because they had lost someone, too. I believe his faith as well as his ability to have gratitude in a dark night allowed his heart to remain open and have forgiveness.

This level of gratitude is definitely something that takes time for most of us, so do what you can when you can. It's about progress, not perfection.

## When In A Dark Place

If you're struggling right now, can you **be grateful for simply being alive?** In every moment of your day, someone will transition to the next journey. Can you be grateful that you're living?

I'll be honest; I don't feel I'm there yet with having gratitude for simply being alive. I have only known two people, my dear second mother Sybil Rhodes, and my nephew Max, who wake up excited to be alive each and every day. They both believe every day is awesome no matter what. I'm working to be more like them. Although Sybil has passed, I believe she's just as excited about life on the other side.

**You might just be in a place where you truly can't be grateful. That's o.k.** When I was grieving, I didn't do my daily gratitude practice. I was simply incapable most days. Every so often I'd be able to say I was grateful for Tony and the cats. I knew I'd return to it when I was ready. The key is to be honest with yourself. Are you really in a space where you can't, such as grieving a loss, or is it something else?

Having gratitude can be easy to forget. Most of us are caught up in our lives, busy, focusing on accomplishing goals, taking care of others, and trying to get it all done. Can you push the pause button and appreciate the life you're living?

I accept where I am and because I'm committed, I keep having more gratitude, feeling more love, and expanding and opening my heart.

·

If you were to ask me what one chapter from this book I'd hope you would incorporate into your life, it would be this one. I often assign this as homework to clients and share as a tip when I give interviews. Being grateful can have a positive and profound impact on your life.

Summary

Develop a daily gratitude practice and see how you're able to deepen it over time. Try and love what is right now. Acknowledge when you're in a challenging space and trust you'll get back to the practice when you're able.

Be grateful for each and every day you have as none is promised to any of us.

→ **Take Actions:**

- Decide what your daily gratitude practice will be.
- Commit to practicing being thankful for 21 consecutive days.
- Look for gratitude in challenging situations.
- Practice loving everything as it is.
- Accept whatever life gives you.
- Share your gratitude.
- Encourage others to share what they appreciate.

# Chapter 18

## Simplify

*Do less and gain more.*

One of the self-care steps I've begun doing, and I encourage my clients to do, is to simplify life. Every New Year, I examine my entire life to find where I can do less, cut something out, or downsize.

I know I'm probably not alone when it comes to doing too much. I used to jam-pack my workday and weekends making sure every minute was counted for and scheduled. I'd try to attend every networking event, meeting, and every interview opportunity, and this was all in addition to coaching, decluttering, organizing, running my business, and trying to live life. It was too much and I was on the path to having a meltdown. I was overwhelmed, frustrated, stressed out, and unhappy. I dreaded all the to-dos that had to be completed every single day. This created more anxiety and worry trying to figure out how to get it all done.

After coming home, dripping with sweat from an outdoor networking event in July, I finally drew a line. I told myself, "Enough!" and recalibrated my life. When I was contemplating why I tried to pack so much in a day, I realized I was driven solely by fear. What if I missed the perfect client? Would a customer be angry if I didn't attend her event? Would I be losing out and miss valuable knowledge? What if this interview could launch my books into the stratosphere? I had to take a deep breath and trust that I'd get what I needed when I needed it. For example, if I didn't make it to every networking event, customers would find their way to me.

As I began to do this, I was more in the flow of life and to-dos were done more quickly and with more ease. I was less stressed and happier. If I missed an event, I trusted it wasn't the right place at the right time for me. I became more in tune with my inner wisdom and started to make choices from a more soulful place. This transferred from my professional to my personal life as well.

*Judy was the kind of mom you could always call for anything. Whatever the task, it was accomplished on time and on point. It was great if you were the one who needed help, but not so much for Judy. She went through life in a perpetual frazzled state because she said yes to everything. Even though she was exhausted and close to tears most days, Judy felt guilty any time she even thought about saying no.*

*We worked first on figuring out why she felt she needed to do so much for everyone all the time. Judy shared that she was afraid to let anyone down. Because her mother had been disappointed so many times by so many people, Judy was on high alert to make sure she never let her down. Judy adopted this tactic for all of her relationships because she witnessed how depressed her mother became. The last thing Judy wanted was to cause anyone pain.*

*As Judy began to release her unrealistic expectations for herself, including that she was responsible for other people's happiness, we looked to how she could simplify her life. Some of her steps included buying store cupcakes for school birthdays instead of making homemade, making enough food for leftovers and getting everyone on board to eat the same meal twice, implementing routines, and simplifying her wardrobe. These little changes had an immediate impact because Judy felt a weight lifted. Judy also noticed that people appreciated her more and offered to help her because she wasn't always overwhelmed or in a hurry.*

What do you need to streamline in life? Does something immediately come to mind or do you need time to contemplate? Is there something driving you crazy right now? How can you simplify your life to release a burden?

## Simplifying Your Life

I consider myself a life organizer and a holistic decluttering professional. It's not just about the physical stuff. There are many ways to streamline your life. It's important to discover what steps you can take and **what can work best for you.** Maybe you can't downsize right now, but you can declutter your garage. Perhaps you can't hire an assistant full time, but you can delegate chores to your children at home. Maybe it's mandatory to attend PTA meetings, but you don't have to volunteer to work registration or bring a snack.

Consider this a starting point of ways to simplify. Make a game out of it. Get your spouse/partner/friend or the family involved. My thoughts for simplifying:

*Declutter.* You probably knew this was coming. When you clear your physical clutter it means fewer items to think about and fewer objects to maintain. Reference Chapter 1 on *Let's Get Physical* for more tips. This whole book is about clearing clutter in many areas of your life, but it's only the tip of the iceberg. Life is simplified on so many levels when you clear your clutter: less time and stress dealing with your physical objects. You may experience better health by cooking more homemade meals in a decluttered kitchen, and can have better sleep when your bed isn't pilled high with stuff.

Remember to **look at all areas of your life to declutter**. Where can you clear your schedule and reduce commitments? What relationships leave you exhausted and who do you need to hang out with less? What can you do to reduce your mental stress?

*Get organized.* Being organized can save you time and money and make life easier all around. If you know where your car keys are each morning, finding them is easy and causes no stress. Life can become effortless. You don't have to be Martha Stewart because this is unrealistic for most people (including me), but make an effort to bring some organization into your life.

I believe one of the most important parts about organization is to **make sure that you take into account your lifestyle and needs**. For instance, in my contact list, I organize phone numbers by first name because that's what works best for me. Some professional organizers would say I'm doing it "wrong". Don't get caught up in what the experts tell you; do what works best for you. If you need some support, hire a professional organizer. Many professionals, including me, work virtually, so even if you're in an area that doesn't have a professional organizer, you can find support. Organizing simplifies your life.

*Downsize.* Begin to look at the physical stuff in your home that you can release. If you want to go all out, see if you can downsize enough to move into a smaller home. This doesn't have to be a tiny house because that isn't for everyone. But if the kids are grown, can you go from 4,000 square feet to 2,000? It can be done.

If you need to begin slowly, comb through your collections. If you collect cookbooks, can you cull your group by selling, donating books to the library, or giving them to a friend who is looking for new recipes? Keep what you really love or consider digitizing everything so you have fewer books in your space. If you're really struggling to release some of your collections, see if you can find a bartering or sharing community or place to rent items.

Another area where you can get some bang for your buck is by letting go of your Tupperware/storage/plastic containers. This is an area many tend to collect and not purge often. Pull out only what you use regularly. Donate the rest. If you no longer garden regularly, give your tools to someone who does or to a community gardening program.

Don't forget to **downsize in non-physical areas.** What fear can you downgrade? If you're afraid you'll let something go and then need it, what options can you come up with to help ease that fear?

What else in your life can you downsize?

*Delegate.* What can you hand off to someone? How can you get children involved in age-appropriate chores? Can you have someone walk the cat or dog or can you contract with a meal service if you're really busy?

If you're challenged delegating because you don't trust people, begin small. Having your child assemble the salad, using a grocery delivery service, or asking the vet to cut the cat's toenails aren't likely to have dire consequences.

You can hire a college or high school student to help with chores or business tasks such as posting to social media or setting up an app. **Consider chores you aren't especially fond of (ironing anyone?) and see who can get it done.**

As you begin to relax and trust more, you can delegate tasks that are more important.

*Automate.* When you find the right technology that works for you, it can make a significant difference. You can set up monthly payments for utilities and memberships, or set up reminders on your phone. You may choose to establish monthly deliveries for goods and services that you use most. We have a monthly shipment for cat food that I can't always find locally. Streamlining those things you have to do every month gives you more time to do the things you desire.

Bonus: many of these you can **"set and forget" or have reminders.** I get a notice a few days before the cat food ships so I can always make changes.

*Schedule less.* I mentioned earlier that I used to be the Queen of Overscheduling. Figure out which appointments, commitments, and meetings you can cut out. Maybe you don't have to go to every board meeting and can get a summary from a colleague. Be discerning when invited to events; what do you really desire to attend? If you get in a good four hours at the gym every week, can you delete the fifth hour? I once worked at a job that had an emergency every hour and consequently, I couldn't get work done. I had to literally keep my schedule open for emergencies. I now keep my schedule open for opportunities. Simplifying my schedule has allowed me to be interviewed in front of new audiences because my schedule wasn't packed so tightly.

Go through your schedule and see **what you can eliminate for the week.** Review any standing commitments and see if you can let any go. When scheduling, check in with yourself. Can you delegate or delete? How important is the event or meeting? Be your own gatekeeper and only schedule what matters most.

★*TIP: If you struggle to say no or easily overcommit, block off random times so you can honestly answer no because you already have an engagement and can't attend.*

*Mindfulness.* This is one of the best tools for simplifying your life. A regular mindfulness practice can calm and clear your mind to understand what's most important to you. If your mind is clutter free it's easier to focus and create what you desire. A regular practice helps keep you centered and grounded. You may find you're in the flow of life more and your to-dos get completed more easily.

This is something to have fun with when exploring. **Experiment and try different practices.** Mowing the lawn is a time for me to do a brain dump and find peace. One friend uses classical music to soothe his mind. Another friend uses a guided meditation app.

There are lots of great mindfulness apps out there like Headspace, Buddhify, Calm, Smiling Time, Meditation Timer Pro, The Mindfulness App, and more. These can help you squeeze in your daily practice when you're on the go or need some guidance.

*Routines.* Routines build good habits, increase efficiency by getting more done in less time, and can simplify life by easing your mind and reducing stress. Routines help you focus to get what really matters done. You save time if you do tasks regularly instead of letting everything pile up.

Look at where you can create **morning, evening and weekend routines.** Here are some examples for morning routines: setting an intention for the day, eating a good breakfast, doing dinner preparation, and double checking the weather before you leave the house.

Evening routines may include reviewing your schedule for the next day, laying out clothes, writing in your gratitude journal, packing your lunch and snacks, and setting your alarm.

Your weekend routines might include errands, chores, decluttering and organizing, family time, you time, spouse time, and meal prep for the week.

Set up routines for your children and family as well.

*Disengage.* We aren't meant to go 24/7. When was the last time that you read a book? Sat and watched a sunset? Spent time in nature? Had a real conversation where no one takes pictures or checks messages? Take the time to be present.

Taking a break from **the digital world isn't the only area in your life that you may need to evaluate.** Do you need to have a time out with any of your relationships? I frequently unfollow people on Facebook who are argumentative or negative the majority of the time.

Can you step back from any worries of the moment? If you know you need to lose weight, can you cut yourself some slack and enjoy a dessert and stop reading all about diets? Would you benefit from taking a week off from the gym? Be honest when you're able to recommit or decide if you need help.

**Release your distractions.** Refer to Chapter 10 *Unplugging* for more guidance.

*Prioritize.* Clearing your clutter is all about focusing on what's significant. Many times you waste time on the busyness of life and don't focus on what's important. If you're clear about what you need and choose to focus on, you can let the less important to-dos go.

My friend Maple was very crafty. She had a 14 x 14 room filled with a variety of creative projects. I suggested she pick three areas she had the time and energy to commit to *right now.* Maple chose soap making, oil painting, and aromatherapy. We put aside all the items for those three projects and decluttered the rest. Simplifying allowed Maple to spend her energy on what she was most interested in doing in the present moment.

Set a deadline if you're feeling stuck and confused. If you say reading *Newsweek* is important, give yourself a month to see how important it really is. If after a month, you haven't read an issue, stop your subscription. You may think that reading *Newsweek* was a priority, but **your actions tell you it wasn't**. If following the news is important, consider a website you can read on your tablet or get alerts sent to your email. Then go back to the drawing board to continue to prioritize your life.

*Release knee jerk reactions.* What makes you respond from a purely emotional place? When do you seem to over or under respond to an event? Where are you, in the past or future, when you are on autopilot and are not living in the present? Knee jerk reactions are based on past experiences. Clearing out your automatic responses to life's events allows you to simplify your life because **many times these reactions end up creating more trouble**, making you lose peace of mind and precious energy, and feel like crap.

For me, it happens in traffic. Thankfully, I'm a lot better than I used to be. Ten years in Los Angeles surrounded by traffic all the time is enough to rile even the calmest person. I'd get bent out of shape, fume, and become angry every time I sat in traffic. This wasn't fun for anyone in the car. I began to practice deep breathing and releasing my frustrations in the gym.

I also had a bad habit of saying "sorry" by default even

when it wasn't my fault and I had no reason to apologize. I'd apologize unnecessarily because of feeling guilty, lacking self-confidence, or trying to be the peacemaker. My automatic response was to immediately soothe the situation and apologizing was the quickest way I knew to accomplish my goal. I own it when I make a mistake or hurt someone, but otherwise I've stopped apologizing.

Instead of losing your mind, **can you take ten deep breaths and let something go?** How else can you release your frustrations? When you slip into autopilot what action can you take in the moment to become present?

It's always worthwhile to do a little soul searching to get to the root of your reaction so you can dissolve it completely and replace it with a new habit or thought.

*Straightforward relationships.* The older I've gotten, the more selective I've become with whom I spend my time. I was never "popular", but I've always had a solid group of close friends. When I met my husband that was also a turning point for me because I discovered that I had some friendships that were less deep and more casual than I thought.

I choose to **spend my time with people who support me, tell me the truth, and love me unconditionally.** I had hoped that the women's group I mentioned earlier in the book would provide spiritual support and friendship, but it didn't. I made the mistake of staying longer than I should have. Recently, I left a Facebook group because it wasn't meeting my needs and there was a lot of complaining.

I'm really conscious of the people I have in my life. While I don't view people as "good" or "bad" as I believe we're all on a path of learning, it's vital to my health and sanity only to spend time with **people who are supportive and are working to become the best versions of themselves.** None of them is perfect by any stretch, but they're working on healing and moving forward.

You don't need 1,000 friends to be happy. Be discerning, simplify, and spend time with those that support you and love you unconditionally. While you can form friendships on line, I don't believe they beat what you can create in real life.

*Say no.* Are you the person people always come to when they need something done because they know you won't say no? Do you often say yes to something you don't want to do? Have you found yourself angry after committing to something that you said you'd never do again?

Many people struggle with saying no. **If you don't say no you can create tons of clutter in your life.** You create emotional clutter with anger for doing something you were against. Physical clutter happens when you can't say no to storing stuff for others; spiritual clutter by not honoring what your soul needs; mental clutter by beating yourself up by ruminating about the woulda coulda shouldas; relationship clutter because you aren't spending time with supportive people; and possible financial clutter by loaning money when you can't say no.

Tips for saying no:

- Practice saying no in front of the mirror or with a trusted friend.
- Be clear and direct. Don't hem and haw.
- Be brief. You don't owe anyone an explanation.
- Say you're not able to commit right now.
- State that you're honored, but can't do it.
- Don't apologize.
- Create a rule. For example, if someone asks you for free advice say, "I wish I could, but I don't offer advice outside of a coaching session."
- Refer someone else you believe may be interested.
- Have a friend support you.

Being able to say no is about good boundaries. If someone gets upset when you say no, it isn't your problem. People that respect you will respect your boundaries. Let the others go.

*Streamline cooking.* I purchased a MealthyPot (pressure cooker) and it has saved me time by being able to prepare meals much more quickly. I love that I can make my own food instead of relying on pre-packaged or processed junk. I can throw in dry beans and have tasty beans not from a can. I know people that really go all out and have more than one pressure cooker so they can do breakfast and dinner in them. You can also use a crockpot to throw everything in the morning and come home with dinner ready.

What kitchen gadgets can you release? Here are 9 of the least used kitchen gadgets[15]: garlic peeling mat, corn cob holders, bread maker, fondue set, chocolate fountain, hand mixer, French press, meat slicer, and toasted sandwich maker. Remember, this is one list I'm citing. I've also read that ice cream machines, pizza cutters, and propane torches aren't used. I personally use my hand mixer a lot. Be honest about what kitchen gadgets you aren't using and release this kitchen clutter.

What other kitchen tools can you use to simplify your life? If the devices would really help you, use them. For instance, Hiku helps you create grocery lists and CuisinartSmarTrack storage claim their containers preserve leftovers before they go bad.

**Apps may help you simplify, too.** Timer+ is a free timer that can run multiple countdowns at the same time while Pepperplate organizes recipes, creates shopping lists, and plans meals based on recipes.

### The Holidays

Are you overwhelmed every holiday season? Have you considered running away from it all just to avoid all the stress the holidays bring? Do you love the holidays but find they have gotten away from the true spirit?

The holidays are a wonderful time for simplifying your life. They are also a time when I see a lot of people stressed out instead of enjoying the season. When you're happy, healthy, and less stressed, everyone wins.

Here are a few ways to streamline the season.

- *Embrace imperfect.* One year, I sent out a Christmas card with a typo. I refused to spend the time or money correcting my mistake. No one ever said anything to me and I lived to share the tale. Life is messy and not picture perfect, so if the pie burns, laugh about it, and get back to enjoying yourself.

- *Do less.* Send an email holiday card instead of printing and mailing a batch. Bake one cookie instead of five different kinds for hostess gifts. Attend fewer parties. Where are you really miserable, overbooked, and overloaded? Take the time to cull and concentrate on what brings you the most joy.

- *Reduce giving gifts.* Save yourself a headache and ask what people want. Buy less, buy used, or don't give gifts. Go though your list and see whom you can eliminate. Do you and your college roommate really need to exchange gifts? Can you get a used treadmill instead of buying a new one? How about creating a new tradition of picking from a hat and giving one nice gift to one person instead of a gift for everyone?

- *Be green or eco friendly.* Repurpose, repair, reduce, reuse, and recycle. Going green saves you time and money and can be fun. For decorations look to the outside (pinecones and garlands) and what you may already have on hand (popcorn) instead of more plastic junk made in China. Set up a recycling center at your party. When entertaining, buy juice in bulk instead of small juice boxes for kids.

- *Smiles, hugs, and encouragement.* These are free and can really make a difference to someone during the holidays. What little acts of kindness can you do to spread cheer? Maybe you can leave water and snacks for delivery and mail workers, buy presents for a family in need, or buy a meal for a homeless person?

- *Reflection and gratitude.* What makes you feel grateful? Who do you truly appreciate? How can you bring that into your life year round? When you do this you buoy your spirits and can reduce your stress. You see the insignificant for what it is and concentrate on what you value most.

Where else can you simplify? Relationships? Clothes? Finances? Health? The more you simplify the easier life becomes.

Summary
Figure out where you can streamline your life. When you simplify your life you gain peace of mind and get more done in less time.

→ Take Actions:

- Reflect on where and what you need to cull in your life.
- Create a list of ways you'd like to streamline.
- Consult and get input from family.
- Recruit support for restructuring your life.
- Review your list: have you examined all areas of your life?
- Decide where you can simplify for the holidays.
- Examine any resistance to streamlining and try to figure out why you resist.

# Chapter 19

## Taking Stock

*Examine your life to be the most awesome version of you.*

Have you ever wondered out loud, "Where did the days/weeks/months/years go?" Do you ever feel like the end of the year sneaked up on you and you haven't accomplished what you set out to, scratching your head and wondering why? Many times you're unaware of your shortcomings and that you need to make a course correction.

What is a life inventory? It's a wonderful tool to support you in realizing where you are in life, what your shortcomings and strengths are, and it can help you focus. When you're clear about who you are and who you aren't, it allows you to release your physical, mental, emotional, and spiritual clutter that doesn't fit who you are now or who you desire to become.

*Mary was extremely overweight. Each year she would gain between five and ten pounds. Mary knew that she needed to lose weight but she'd push her health aside, vowing to address it later. Her doctor had encouraged Mary to diet and exercise. Mary always said she'd get to it "someday" but someday never came.*

*After a decade of not losing weight, eating well, or exercising, at 48 Mary had a heart attack. It was the wake-up call she needed to realize that she had to make some serious changes. Had Mary done a life inventory, and been honest, she might have acknowledged that her physical health needed to be a priority. By beginning to lose weight and finding the support she needed, Mary could have discovered that she overate to suppress her grief of losing a child. At an attempt to face her pain, she ate. Mary needed to process her grief and become present instead of using food as comfort.*

*Mary also took the bold step of admitting that at times she wanted to die. Perhaps unconsciously she was trying to achieve that by overeating. Completing a life inventory supported Mary in realizing she couldn't handle everything on her own and needed help. She not only found guidance through a dietician but also found a grief support group.*

*I recently coached Cathy who was a self-proclaimed mean girl. She was brave enough to say "I don't like this about myself, how can I change?" Cathy had shared that she had tormented girls all throughout school. "I was shy and insecure. Being a bully was my way of covering that up and I'd strike out before someone could hurt me." When she went away to college, Cathy figured this would be a good time to start new. While she wasn't as mean as she was in high school, Cathy had a biting sarcasm and no one wanted to be at the end of her barbs.*

*When she was graduated from college, Cathy lost touch with her closest friends and chalked it up to distance. As she began to form new friendships as a young adult, Cathy's armor went up and once again became harsh. One day, Cathy had a minor crisis and reached out to several friends. None of them came to her aid. She didn't understand and angrily confronted one of the last women she contacted. Her friend responded, "Cathy, I'm sorry, but I don't consider you a good friend. You're always defensive and unkind most of the time. While it may be good for a laugh or two when it's gentle ribbing, you always go for the kill." Cathy was stunned. After some reflection, she knew she had to make some changes.*

*When Cathy came to me we discussed why she was a mean girl. In her household growing up, being unkind was par for the course. The cruelest person usually got his or her way and being harsh was a way of survival. We devised a plan how she could better fulfill her needs instead of lashing out at others. When Cathy thought about her life, she realized that she'd never had many close friends because she was so busy bulldozing over them.*

*Then Cathy made a very brave move. She contacted former friends, explaining she was working on being a better woman, and asked them to share how she was as a friend and what they thought of her. Some of the comments were hard to hear, but the feedback ultimately helped Cathy get a clear picture of her actions and how she could change.*

By being truthful and asking yourself challenging questions, you can course correct. What will you discover about yourself? Remember, a life inventory isn't just about acknowledging your weaknesses; it's also about finding out your strengths, passions, and challenges.

If you're struggling with your life inventory, consider working with a professional. Don't do this with a friend or family member who judges you or shares your innermost thoughts with others. This is a road map to wellness and you need to be 100% honest with yourself and your tribe needs to support you 100%.

Taking an inventory of your life **allows you to get a clear, frank picture of where you are.** I've not always had healthy relationships and often gave without receiving. By taking an inventory, I faced my challenges and released my unhealthy relationships.

### Where Am I?

This can be painful, so be very gentle with yourself. If you can't acknowledge a problem, you can't fix it. You purchased this book because you're choosing to change your life. Honor that by committing to a candid inventory. This is a wonderful exercise to pass along to a friend, spouse, child, or family member as well.

Consider also completing a family inventory with your spouse/partner and children. I'd encourage you to do these evaluations annually. Once you set up the framework, it will be easy to check in with yourself and contemplate questions and choose the direction you'd like to go.

We're taught subjects like reading, writing, and arithmetic in schools, yet not how to live a full and enriched life. How often have you asked yourself, "How can I be a better person?" "How can I improve my life?" "What are my weaknesses?" or "What are my challenges?"

I encourage you to write down your thoughts after contemplating. **Putting ink to paper and seeing it in black and white helps you take action.** If you try to keep it in your head, you may not remember everything and you can't easily review what you're thinking. Whether it's in a notebook, app, the guided workbook, or Word document, gathering your feelings and beliefs in one place will support you in working through the questions. The companion workbook to

*Clear Your Clutter Inside & Out* can guide you not only with this chapter, but also all the chapters of this book.

### Evaluation

How can you best evaluate your life? I'm a fan of journaling and find putting my thoughts on paper really helps me. Because it's just me, I'm in a headspace where I can be honest and non-judgmental. Below are some categories with a few questions in each. At the end of the book, I provide a more comprehensive list of questions you may want to consider.

*Relationships.* Are my relationships mainly give and take or are they out of balance? Why do I allow people to cross my boundaries?

*Health.* Do I eat mainly healthy foods or mainly eat fast food, take out, and junk food? Am I able to effectively handle stress or does it make me ill?

*Finances.* Am I able to mainly save, and spend when necessary or do I overspend or hoard my money? Do I have a plan for the future or live paycheck to paycheck?

*Emotions.* Am I mainly happy and at peace or sad and angry? Do I process what I'm feeling in a healthy manner or ignore, stuff, and/or avoid my feelings?

*Spirituality.* Am I able to find gratitude in my life mainly or instead focus on everything that is wrong? Do I feel some connection to a higher power, community, or nature, or do I feel isolated and alone?

*Work.* Do I like my career or do I have a job that just

pays the bills? If I could do any job, what would I choose?

*Play.* How well do I enjoy life? Am I able to be playful or do I make everything a competition?

What questions can you add to these categories? What other areas in your life need a thorough examination right now?

Provide as much detail as possible as you answer. **There's no right or wrong, so don't censor yourself.** Consider as many perspectives as possible for the questions. You may also write whatever comes to you immediately and then circle back to the questions to write more after some reflection. You may also want to ask trusted family and friends their thoughts on some of your questions. Sometimes you have a blind spot and can't see where you're challenged or have a talent.

★*TIP: Consider "free writing": simply writing whatever comes to mind. Maybe there's something else your soul is trying to tell you. You may start out thinking that your finances are your biggest concern only to discover it's your health or a relationship. Free writing can also be useful if you're stuck and don't know what to write. Just begin writing and the words will start to come.*

## EXAMPLE:

Q: Do you like your career or do you have a job that just pays the bills?

*I've been thinking about this question for a bit. My immediate answer was I have a career!!! But when I took the*

234

*time to really think about it, I have a job. I'm grateful for the benefits and that it does pay my bills. I do like my job, but it's not my passion. I'm not sure what I really desire to do, but I'd like to be more excited about work and waking up happy that it's Monday morning. I want to do something where I'm making a difference. My strengths are photography, graphic arts, and editing. I enjoy being creative, designing, and interacting with people. I've always been curious and amazed by nature. Oh, and I could spend all day hanging out with kids. I'm drawn to their openness and sense of wonder.*

Don't view this as a deadline driven assignment. Think about the questions. I do believe that our first answers are usually our "best" and come from an intuitive place. Perhaps you ask yourself a question such as "Do I love myself?" and the first answer that pops up is "Yes, but I allow people in my life who don't love me." Write down what comes to mind and you can toss it around and come back to answer more fully. It might take you a month or two to answer some questions. Just get started! Maybe you're in a relationship that's not healthy and loving and you haven't been able to admit it. I believe your soul is always speaking to you; it's whether or not you're consciously choosing to listen. Hopefully, taking a life inventory gets you more in touch and in tune with your inner spirit.

Keep moving forward each day to answer questions. Take a break when you feel you need to, but I suggest not staying away too long. Be aware and understand if you truly need a break or if you're procrastinating. Procrastinating is usually about fear, so that may be a starting point for you: "What am I afraid I may discover if

I do my life inventory?"

After responding to your questions, review your answers and pick one area for improvement. (While you can do more, I suggest starting out slowly. If you're really ready to go, choose no more than three. You want to make a few changes well, not do several improvements so-so.) **Contemplate what really bothers you *right now*.** Will there be negative consequences if something doesn't change immediately? What are you inspired to change? Keep your master list but make a short list of one or two areas you can work on changing now.

Don't expect change to happen overnight and don't try to tackle everything in one week. Record what you practice. Make notes of how you felt, what worked and what didn't, and what else you may need to try. Think of yourself as an archeologist or researcher on a treasure hunt of self-discovery for what works best for you.

## EXAMPLES:

*I had been avoiding going to my family doctor because I don't want to know if I'm sick. I finally went to see her because I'm tired of being exhausted all the time. They did blood work to rule out medical issues and I'm waiting for the results. In the meantime, I'm taking a class on healthy eating. I also signed up for tai chi to see if that helps.*

*Three times this week I exploded over really stupid stuff. It made me push pause. I realized I have a lot of buried anger but I have no idea where it comes from or what it's about. I need help in figuring out what it is so I can let it go. I've contacted three therapists and am interviewing them this week. When I find a good fit, I'll commit to weekly appointments.*

Can you notice any time that an unhealthy behavior has helped you? You rarely take action that doesn't benefit you in some way. For your next step, use the item you've decided to tackle, or pick another one from your life inventory. Explore what benefit you received from a certain behavior or incident.

I was recently struggling with someone who hurt me. I was very upset and directed my anger at him. While he was unkind, I had to look within in order to release my pain. After further examination, I realized that by being angry with him, I avoided being angry with myself. I didn't want to face that I had made a really dumb decision and be upset with myself. With this knowledge, I released my anger not only at my friend but also myself. Had I not done self-examination, I'd have missed this gift.

## EXAMPLES:

*Finally addressing my tiredness, instead of continuing to avoid it, was a gift because I discovered I have Epstein Barr Virus, also known as mono. EBV can leave you tired for weeks or months. I'm resting, taking care of myself, and making my health a priority. I'm making plans to improve my health even more once I'm better.*

*With the help of a therapist, I was able to discover what really angered me. I was upset with myself about staying too long in a relationship that wasn't going anywhere. I'm angry that I was too afraid to leave for so long. I realized I'm afraid to be alone and need to have compassion towards myself. Along with the gift of self-compassion, I realized how isolated I'd become and am making real efforts to reconnect with friends and seek out new supportive friendships. I ended up meeting a really cool woman and we're writing a play together.*

As you continue to move forward, make longer-term goals to take action for changes. Look back to the *Introduction* at the beginning of the book about taking action. Review how to create SMART goals and other tips for success.

**Don't be ashamed to get help.** Many times you're taught to go it alone and figure it out by yourself because it's important to be "independent". This book is meant as a beginning to get you to understand where you have clutter and what steps you can take to improve your life. While you may be able to easily clear declutter in one area, you may struggle in others. Honor the places where you need support.

Summary
Completing a life inventory allows you to make sure you don't sleepwalk through life and can show you where you need to course correct. Evaluate where you are with honest answers and take time to thoroughly complete your list of questions.

➔Take Actions:

- Create a list of questions for your life inventory.
- Complete a life inventory.
- Examine how your actions and behaviors benefited you.

- Pick one area you'd like to change.
- Commit to course correcting.
- Find an accountability partner or people with similar goals to help keep you focused.
- Review your life plan annually.

# Chapter 20

## Gossip Girl

*When you judge another, you judge yourself.*

When you gossip, you create clutter in your life. Gossip brings you out of the present moment as you focus on past events. When you share, or listen, to stories about others, you bring that negativity into your life. You can also create karmic clutter by spreading falsehoods that could have a direct impact on someone's life. Sharing rumors about others is judgmental and often leads you to make unfair or false assumptions about people.

*One New Year's Eve a friend of mine, Marti, had a little too much to drink. In loud whispers Marti shared with me that she thought a married friend of ours, Gene, was having an affair. She proceeded to tell me all the "juicy" details. I was too stunned at first to respond. When she finished I asked her how she'd feel if someone said that about her husband. Marti tottered off in her drunken state and I hoped she wouldn't repeat this gossip.*

*I was surprised because Marti and her husband were very good friends with Gene and his wife. I was shocked, angry, and confused. Why would Marti share this? Whether or not Gene was having an affair, it was none of our business. If Gene were guilty, he'd have to face the consequences with his wife. I was close enough to Marti to know that she and her husband were having problems. Gossiping about Gene wouldn't improve her relationship with her husband. At best, it would make Marti feel temporarily better about herself and possibly her marriage.*

*When we left the party, I said to my husband, "If Marti is spreading rumors about Gene, imagine what she's saying about us." I began to get uncomfortable and worried. While I've committed no criminal acts, I shared very personal thoughts and feelings with Marti. How can you gossip about someone in your inner circle?*

*While there were other contributing factors, Marti and I are no longer friends. After that New Year's Eve party, I knew I couldn't trust her. I wouldn't feel comfortable sharing my authentic self with someone who might turn around and mock me or share my most personal trials and tribulations with others.*

While some may dismiss this as a drunken moment, I believe more often than not the truth comes out when you've had too much to drink. What if Gene's wife overheard? She would have been hurt, as Gene would have. Perhaps it could have planted a seed of distrust between Gene and his wife.

Even if it were true and Gene was having an affair, it wasn't Marti's place to share. Gene was a well-known businessman in the area. If other people heard he was having an affair, they might stop doing business with him. Sometimes the consequences of our actions can't be known ahead of time.

Gossip can also do more than hurt someone's feelings or cause tension in a relationship. Workplace gossip can also have harsh repercussions. I had a friend, Lisa, who was a professor at a local college. A jealous colleague, Frank, spread false rumors about her. Lisa was upset, angry, and frustrated but chose not to take any action. Lisa figured that if she rose above Frank's pettiness that he would stop and the scuttlebutt would die down.

A few months later, Lisa was denied tenure. After talking with some other professors, Lisa believes Frank's unfounded accusations contributed, and if not were the sole reason, to Lisa not receiving tenure. She is now in arbitration and is using what Frank said as evidence that she was denied permanent status as a professor. While there are many pieces to being tenured, the gossip did make the rounds and it would be hard to deny that the rumors didn't play a part.

As I was finishing the final edits for this book, a woman I knew was killed. While we weren't close, I was shocked and saddened by some of the comments I saw on social media. This woman was a mother, daughter, friend, and at any time those closest to her could have read these mean spirited and public comments. I think too often we forget **there are real people behind the face and name you see online.** Her family and friends had barely started grieving when the rumor mill was in full force.

Gossiping
If you think others might want you to gossip, you're right. Gossip makes magazines sell and viewers visit websites. On my iPad news feed there are sites such as Page 6 even though I didn't add them. Luckily, I figured out how to unfollow. Gossip has now become part of the mainstream media. Celebrity gossip is a $3 billion a year industry according to The Week[16].

Take a moment to reflect. **How do you participate in celebrity gossip?** Do you chat with your friends about what you hear? Do you read online gossip sites? How much do you spend—say a subscription to People magazine—to stay current with gossip?

Let's examine gossip and ways we can release this spiritual clutter.

## Work Scuttlebutt

Gossip seeps into our professional lives. It was reported by a Social Issues Research Center that gossip accounts for 55% of men's conversation time and 67% of women's.[17]

At work gossip has been found to:

- Reduce productivity as time is wasted.
- Compromise professional standards.
- Create pain, resentment, and distrust.
- Waste energy finding out who said what.
- Diminish confidence in management if it continues.[18]

While most gossip might be viewed as harmless, it can be very detrimental. If two people are vying for a promotion, one can leak gossip for a competitive edge. Or someone may not get a promotion, or even be fired, based on false rumors like my friend Lisa's experience.

Do you gossip at work? Are you closest to people who share the latest rumors? How can participating in the office scuttlebutt be not only harming your work performance but also how others view you? **Have you ever heard gossip about a colleague only to find** out later that it was untrue? Have workplace rumors ever cost you anything? Be honest with yourself. Don't judge your actions, but rather acknowledge them so you can change.

### Frenemies?

Do you gossip about friends? Have you broken a confidence? Do you tend to gossip about the same person? What you see as innocuous could actually be damaging.

I had a neighbor tell me a home in our neighborhood was in foreclosure. I had zero judgment about this, but was concerned. Foreclosures can negatively affect the price of our home and we'd be putting our house on the market soon. Instead of taking this gossip as truth, I went to an open house and asked the realtor. I was very straightforward and told him I heard this from a neighbor. I was happy to find out the home had not gone into foreclosure.

What if that scuttlebutt went around the neighborhood and word reached that neighbor's employer? **Someone's reputation can be damaged on false information.** Pause to consider if you ever hurt someone by gossiping or sharing unfounded information.

When has gossip hurt you? Have you lost a friendship because you or your friend spread rumors? Has it cost you anything such as your reputation at work? How did it feel to be on the receiving end? Did you confront the person or let it slide? Would you have done anything differently?

★*TIP: Remove gossip sites and apps from your phone and social media feeds. Unfollow or unfriend people always spreading and sharing rumors and scuttlebutt.*

### Why Do We Gossip?

Probably most of you have gossiped at one time or another. I know I have. You may share rumors if you're jealous. **Perhaps you use gossip to manipulate or control others.** You may also spread scuttlebutt because you see knowledge as power. A dear friend of mine shared that she recently gossiped because she was insecure.

I know for myself that I read gossip to feel better about myself and to have a focal point for my frustrations. I'd think I'm not as bad as those crazy housewives of Orange County or New York. I may not be wealthy, but at least I'm not acting like a fool in public.

When you focus on the faults of others, how can you expect others not to do the same to you? **Whatever you put out in the world comes back to you in some way, shape, or form.** When you take delight in mean comments about others, couldn't your time be better spent working on yourself? Why not spend the time improving your own life or supporting others instead of bringing them down? Putting someone else down doesn't raise you up. In fact, in lowers your vibration. Ever since I quit reading gossip I feel a lot better about myself.

Gossip may also be used as a tool to bond. Have you ever stood around the water cooler at work talking about the latest celebrity divorce? Don't feel shame if you have, just become aware of when you easily slip into chattering about others. How do you feel afterwards? Do you still feel connected? Perhaps you may feel that the connection over talking about a colleague was a fleeting bonding experience but you may not feel so good later.

Spreading rumors can also be a way to isolate someone. Did you go to high school or college with a "slut"? These women were separated, their character assassinated, and tried without a jury or a judge. The truth seemed irrelevant once someone was branded. Gossiping also made these women easy targets to be bullied.[19]

Or perhaps you saw some of the "popular" crowd control their posse by threatening to share secrets that would surely mean removal from the pack. I had a friend, Heather, who was a successful saleswoman. One of her co-workers, Lyn, gossiped behind her back and tried to get the other associates to gang up against Heather. While it may have made Lyn feel powerful in the moment, in the long run her actions hurt her more than it hurt my friend. Heather continued to rack up sales and her co-workers began to ask her for help to increase their commissions. Lyn was the one who became isolated and eventually quit.

I've seen people argue in favor of gossip, but I stick with my original position that gossip is spiritual clutter and it's a good thing to remove from your life.

## How To Stop
For me, the worst thing about gossip is it breaks a confidence. Someone confided in you and you broke that bond. Probably most of us have had that happen to us. It's not fun.

Like many of your challenges and weaknesses, gossiping is a habit that can be unlearned. Go on a diet from gossip. Better yet, make not participating in rumors a lifestyle change.

Think about **why you listen or contribute to gossip**. Do you lack self-esteem and spread rumors to feel better about yourself? Do you feel you're missing something, like friendship, and use it as a way to connect with others? Are you convinced that it allows you to have power or control over people?

Pick an area where you'd like to stop gossiping. If you really aren't sure what to choose, where do you spend the most time engaging in chatter: with co-workers, reading *People*, perusing celebrity websites, or dishing with friends and family?

Gossiping once in a while is probably the most realistic. That's okay. It's all about moderation. You might be surprised as you being to curb gossiping at **the amount of time and energy you were spending on it**. Here are suggestions to slow down the process of sharing the scuttlebutt and perhaps stopping altogether.

*Cancel your subscription.* If you're someone who likes to read about celebrities, stop reading *People*, *US Weekly*, etc. Bring a book to the doctor's office so you're not tempted to read any magazines. Unfollow people, places, and sites on social media and delete from your feed.

*Put a moratorium on reading online gossip.* I used to read gossip websites for mindless reading to take a break. Then I participated in a weeklong retreat and was only online to check business emails. That gave me the break and incentive I needed to quit. How many spiritual people are hanging out reading rumors about people they don't know? A few months later, I was at the doctor's office and couldn't miss the *People* cover that had just been delivered. I remarked to the receptionist that I was sad to see Ben Affleck and Jennifer Garner were getting a divorce. She looked at me like I had two heads and proclaimed, "What? This has been online and in magazines for months that they were having problems!" This is another example of how prevalent and "normal" gossip is in our society.

*Enlist support.* Ask your friends to support your gossip free zone. Who is your accountability partner to remind you to stop? Tell your gossip buddies that you're on a moratorium and suggest a positive activity such as complementing one another. Figure out what healthy habit with which you can replace gossiping instead of chatting about the drama of others.

*Bond differently.* Ask yourself if there is **a healthier way to bond with people**. For example, you can find common ground with hobbies, sports teams, or food. Make a rule as a group or with your friends that while hanging out you won't delve into gossiping.

*Lend a hand.* Instead of isolating someone through gossip, can you befriend him or her? Who knows? You may discover a new friend. Perhaps you can have an honest conversation with her (or him) and let her know how her behavior may be contributing to others gossiping about her. You can also suggest your friends give someone a chance and to fact check before spreading rumors.

*Cut it out.* Be a trendsetter and stay away from mudslinging. Don't judge those that gossip; instead lead by example and gently ask them to stop. Agree to talk about your favorite T.V. shows, sports teams, or your favorite books. Make a promise to not say anything negative about anyone.

*Be prepared.* With some strategies, it's easier to change your actions. Set a random timer on your phone and see if the timer catches you mudslinging. Block gossip websites on your phone and computer. Have a canned kindness phrase you can instantly repeat when you notice you're spreading rumors. Like anything, it takes practice, but know you can break the gossip habit.

While gossiping may give you temporary relief of problems, or make you feel better about yourself, **it's really wasted time.** You can be devoting precious time working on yourself, engaging in an activity you love, or spending quality time with people you love.

## Summary
If you regularly gossip you can cause harm to others, especially if rumors are particularly negative and untrue. You're a partner in spreading lies and people will trust you less.

## ➔ Take Actions:

- Acknowledge when, where, who, and what causes you to gossip.

- Ask yourself what prompts you to spread rumors.
- Put a moratorium on idle chatter with family, friends, and co-workers.
- Support someone instead of isolating him through mudslinging.
- Quit engaging in workplace scuttlebutt.
- Figure out a healthy habit to replace gossiping.
- Ask yourself how you can improve your life instead of dishing dirt.
- Refuse to gossip.

# Chapter 21

## Space Clearing: Home Sweet Home

*Everything is energy.*

I chose to include a "bonus" chapter on energetic clutter. This might be a weird concept for you, but whether you believe this from a physics or spiritual perspective, everything is energy[20]. Your body is energy as well as this book you're reading and the chair on which you're sitting. You feel energy whether or not you're conscious of it. Energetic clutter can have an unhealthy impact not only on your physical space but also your psyche and can quite literally weigh on you. How your space feels can overwhelm your emotions with sadness, or unbalance your mental health with depression or anxiety, and create spiritual clutter by preventing you from simplifying or seeing all the good you have in life.

Think about, or better yet, walk into, a cluttered room full of books, papers, and knickknacks all crammed together and covered in dust. How does that space feel? Most likely the space has heavy or dense energy, and perhaps a sensation of muck you feel like you need to push through. You might also feel claustrophobic, overwhelmed, or trapped.

Here's another way to view energetic clutter. You probably have heard the expression "The tension was so thick you could cut the air with a knife." **If you walked into a room after an intense argument, you'd most likely feel the unpleasant, or thick, energy.** You might not be able to articulate what you're feeling but you can probably sense a heaviness or density. I doubt that you'd choose to spend a lot of time in a room that felt that way.

Parents get upset when kids have temper tantrums, but actually tantrums are great for removing energetic clutter. Kids instinctively know this is a way of releasing and moving out the unpleasant energy. A happy kid isn't throwing a fit, but an exhausted, overwhelmed, angry child is. If you suppress emotions, they stay stuck and in your energetic field. Emotions are simply energy wanting to be in motion. If you don't release negative feelings in a healthy manner, they will find a way to release, sometimes at the most inopportune times. You're healing when you release undesirable emotions instead of allowing them to fester into a wound.

Prior to starting my own business, I worked for a non-profit that had a lot of intense, draining energy. I dreaded going into work each day. Many people at work were angry, frustrated, and depressed. There always seemed to be a crisis and a few people looked like they'd explode any second. I felt suffocated, stressed out, and tired being in the office and I wasn't alone.

Even people at that non-profit who may not have believed in the concept of energetic clutter knew the space felt yucky. I'd joke that if I brought my singing crystal bowl to the office that it would shatter into a million pieces from all the negative energy. A few years after I left to start my own business, the non-profit went under. I have no doubt the negative feeling of the space contributed to the organization having to close its doors.

*Melissa didn't like to work in her home office even though her space had been decluttered and was well organized. After talking with Melissa and asking questions, we figured out that the space felt suffocating and stagnant to her. It wasn't conducive for creativity or focusing when Melissa was working with clients. "When I'm in my office I feel uncomfortable and everything takes a major effort. I don't feel I can give my best effort and my creativity flounders. I find myself making excuses to not work in my home office." A coffee shop lacked privacy and wasn't a viable solution, especially when she had a dedicated office space at home.*

*I shared with Melissa some ways to do an energetic clearing and then suggested she use sage to clear the room. Melissa also found a candle that lifted her spirits and infused a wonderful fragrance into the room. "I can't get over how different my office feels! It's like it's a whole new space. The area feels joyful, expansive, and open. I can create, serve, and dream here!" Melissa no longer dreads Monday mornings at the office.*

*Because she could see such a significant difference, Melissa committed to energetically cleaning her office, and home, on a regular basis.*

Clearing my space regularly is really important, because I can sense people's energy and what they bring into our space, so I remove energetic clutter on a regular basis. We're often told how welcoming our home feels. To me, **decluttering your energetic space is just as important as clearing your inner and outer clutter.**

Because I've found great benefit from space clearing, I also encourage my clients once they have decluttered to energetically sweep their rooms. You can really have a lot of fun with this. If you're ever feeling blah about your space, this is an easy pick me up that can quickly change and shift the energy of a room.

## Feeling Energy

Even though you can't see energetic clutter, you can feel it. Try to understand that **how your home and office feel can impact your life**. A room that feels closed and has a lot of stuck, stagnant energy can be a magnet for physical clutter. An area that feels good is a place where you choose to be and can buoy your mental, emotional, and spiritual states.

Most women would probably tell you that they've encountered a man who felt slimy. His energy just didn't feel good and they would make a quick exit. It's been my experience that politicians can have an energy that I don't choose to be around. By sensing energy that isn't compatible with yours, you can save yourself time by knowing this probably isn't a person with whom you'd choose to become involved with personally or professionally.

To begin to clear your space, I encourage you to **learn to feel energy**. You can feel energy in different ways. I feel energy through the palms of my hands. I sense a swirling motion that may feel hot or cold. I also sense strong emotions in my body (clairsentience). You may feel a crackling energy or a chilly sensation.

Other ways you can feel energy include: seeing

(clairvoyance); hearing (clairaudience); smelling (clearscent); touching (psychometry or clairtangency); emotions/feelings (clairempathy): and tasting (clairgustance).

To start, I recommend sitting quietly with your eyes closed. Take a deep breath. Place your open palms facing each other. Play around by imagining there is a ball of energy between your palms. Stay with it until you can "feel" the sensations and then begin to push that energy back and forth or wiggle your fingers and feel the force at the tips of your fingers.

Repeat the exercise but now try and feel what is there between your hands. Is it empty space or can you feel the molecules and atoms filling the area?

Next, visualize being surrounded by the lightest of feathers. How does this energy feel? Can you sense the "lightness" of the energy? What other **words would you use to describe what you're feeling and sensing?** Now envision being enveloped by mud. Does this feel cumbersome? How else does being stuck in mud feel for you?

Ask to feel an emotion like anger or sadness. If nothing happens, remember an event that made you feel upset. Are you sensing a feeling? What sensations come to mind? Now attempt this exercise with a feeling such as happiness or joy. Does the air around you seem to shift? Do you feel a difference in your body? Record what sensations, feelings, colors, smells, tastes, or sounds you experience with each exercise.

**Be open, play, and have fun!** This experience is individualized and will be different for everyone.

If you're having trouble feeling energy, take a break. Ask for guidance to be able to sense energy from your angels, God, the Universe, or your Higher/Sovereign Self. Although this can be challenging, it may be easier for you to simply enter the room and feel the energy. Try different ways and practices. If you closed your eyes, try opening them. If you were sitting, try standing. Play around to figure out what works best for you.

★*TIP: Practice feeling energy when you're calm, relaxed, unhurried, in a playful and expansive mood. The more joyful I feel, the easier I sense energy. Release all your expectations and trust you're learning and feeling what you need to know in this moment.*

## Assessing Energy

Now that you've learned to sense energy, it's time to **evaluate the feel of your space.** Do you tend to gravitate towards certain rooms? Are there any areas you avoid? You may choose to start in a space that doesn't feel so great because you're ready to clear it. Or you may decide that you can feel energy better in a room that feels good to you and you're comfortable spending time.

Here are some questions to ask as you get started: What words immediately come to mind when you enter the space? Does the energy of the room feel light and welcoming or stuck and unpleasant? **Do any words pop into your head to describe your sensations?** What do you feel or sense? Are you able to smell, taste or see anything? Does the space have anything it would like to tell you?

If you're feeling unsure, close your eyes and ask, "What do I need to know about this room right now?"

*Rosie described her kitchen as feeling like chaos. She felt the energy was congested and thick and she didn't like to spend time cooking in the kitchen and would eat out a lot. Once Rosie cleared her kitchen, she was comfortable and happy in the space and enjoyed cooking.*

Make a list of all the rooms in your home or office you'd like to assess. I encourage you to **do all the spaces in your home as one area affects another** and your entire home. Clearing one room won't remove all of your energetic clutter.

## Clearing Energetic Clutter

Now that you've assessed each room, it's time for some space clearing to release energetic clutter.

I believe it doesn't matter where you start and I haven't found any difference going clockwise or counter clockwise. However, some people may disagree, so you may choose to do more research. Make sure you clear everywhere, such as corners, in closets, and under beds. If anything feels really yucky, spend more time on it.

Here are some ways you can clear your space. Experiment and see what feels good to you.

*Smoke clearing*[21]. This is when you burn herbs, such as sage or lavender, to clear energetic clutter. Light the stick or use one leaf and clear the room by swirling the stick as you walk around. I use a seashell underneath the bundle to catch any ashes. It does have a smoky scent that I like, but it's a personal preference. I've never set off a fire alarm, but you may choose to open some windows.

*Essential oils.* You can put drops in a spray bottle with purified water and spritz the room. Or take a flower and dip into scented water / essential oil mixture and flick drops around your space. Some of my favorite essential oils are lavender for a calming scent, citrus and peppermint for uplifting and energizing, and frankincense for a sacred smell.

*Sally fell in love with essential oils and experiments with different scents now. She believes experimenting with the oils not only clears her space but also enriches her creative side.*

*Sound.* I have a Tibetan singing brass bowl and a crystal bowl. Sound is a great way to disrupt negative patterns. When I find myself starting to eat emotionally I use sound to dismiss my anxious feelings. You can also go through your home and clap your hands. Bells are an option or any music you love. Don't limit yourself!

*Sea Salt.* You can use sea salt (or create your own with water and salt) and use a flower, or other form of nature, to cleanse the room. Dab the flower in the salt water and release it around the room.

*Incense.* This aromatic material releases a fragrant smoke when burned. Consider lighting incense in another room so you receive an occasional whiff when you're in another area. It comes in cones, sticks, and a variety of scents.

Make this a fun, joyful project. What other methods of space clearing would you like to try?

I also envision in my mind, draining all the energy out of the room. I stand in the room and see four golden roses anchoring the top of the room and four anchoring the bottom of the room. I believe the rose is a universal symbol of love. After I have the roses in place, I imagine gold cords connecting all the roses. Next, I visualize the four top roses all attach and the four bottom roses link together. Then the top and bottom roses become anchored to one another. I then slowly use my hands to drain the energy from the room, moving the energy and my hands down. I visualize the energy draining out of the home, going down into the earth until it reaches the molten core. I see the energy melting into the core, being cleansed, and then become a part of the core to be reused. I do this several times until I feel the energy is clean. When I'm finished, I fill the space with gold or white light from Source.

While clearing my spaces, I focus on what I desire to release (negativity, sadness, fear, or stuck energy). After I've cleared the cluttered energy I also fill up the room with intention. Setting your purpose is powerful. **What is it that you choose to bring into the room?** Happiness, peace, creativity, focus? More joy, light, love?

Before I move into a new home or after I leave a space, I do a thorough space clearing. It allows me to have gratitude for my time at the old home, gain closure, and leave a clean slate for the new owners. I set the intention for a new space and clear the energy of the previous owners before I move my belongings in my new space. You may consider doing the same.

You may be wondering how often you should clear your space. I say whenever it doesn't feel good. I encourage you to record what you felt and what techniques you used when clearing your rooms. Note anything else that you believe is important.

Finally, I trust that I'm doing energetic decluttering "right" and the rooms are cleaned and cleared. I'm not a fan of "one size fits all" with anything, including space clearing. I try different practices, add or delete, and check in about what's needed in the moment. I treat this as a tool for my toolbox and am always on the lookout for something else I can try.

<u>Summary</u>
Everything is energy and you can create energetic clutter that can impact your life. You can feel negative energy even though you can't see it. Clean your space anytime it doesn't feel good.

→ Take Actions:

- Practice feeling energy.
- Record how you best sense vibrations.
- Observe how your space feels in different rooms.
- Experiment with a variety ways to declutter your space.
- Clear your rooms, focusing on what you choose to release.
- Set the intention post clearing and then fill it with love, light, color, or whatever you choose.

# Clear your clutter to create the life you choose, deserve & desire.

# IMMEDIATE TAKE ACTION PLAN

Perhaps you've completed only a few of the chapters or answered every single question in the book as well as created *Take Action* plans. No matter how much you've completed, you may still be thinking, "Dang! I have a lot of clutter. Where do I start?" Even if you've sketched all the actions you need to take, you may be feeling inundated. This next step is designed to help ease your overwhelm.

Review each of the chapters you've completed and highlight what's most immediate or what you feel moved to declutter right now. Record your to-dos below. Refer to the *Take Action* section at the beginning of the book for guidelines for making decisions and creating a successful strategy.

I suggest concentrating on no more than three tasks as you begin the process of clearing your clutter on the inside and out.

## EXAMPLES:

*After reviewing the chapters, I decided that clearing paper clutter is my number one priority. I paid my mortgage late twice this year and need to get paper under control. I'm going to hire a productivity specialist to help me sort it all out and find an organizing system that works. Once I do that, I'll review what else I highlighted that I need to declutter.*

*While my kitchen needs decluttering, I need to get rid of my anxiety first. I posted in my women's group for referrals. I'm making appointments to test drive three therapists and commit to working bi weekly with the right person. After I've begun dealing with my anxiety, I'll make a list of all the steps to declutter my kitchen. I'm nervous about decluttering my kitchen. I'll set a timer for 10 minutes and see how I feel at the end.*

*Looking at all that I need to do, I'm really exhausted and not even sure where to start. I need to get support. I have a lot of unresolved anger. I exploded at the cashier at the grocery store yesterday for no reason. I wasn't angry with her, but I'm not sure what triggered my response. I need professional help. I'll also go to the doctor to make sure nothing is physically wrong with me. I'm really motivated to tackle my challenges and have the time, energy, and money to do so.*

*I'm going to say what I'm grateful for each day because that's something I can easily do. Once I get that routine down, I'll see what else on my list I can tackle. I need to be in a better frame of mind to make any major changes. I'm hopeful increasing my gratitude will help me.*

*I need to take baby steps so I don't become overwhelmed and quit. I'm going to:*

- *Say no to the party next Friday;*
- *Ask John to help me go through our bills; and*
- *Sign up for the Introduction to Bridge class.*

*I'll continue with the baby steps and see how I feel after completing three small to-dos.*

# MY IMMEDIATE TAKE ACTION PLAN

# FINAL THOUGHTS

Whew! You did it! Take time to congratulate, honor, and reward yourself. Completing this book took effort, awareness, courage, time, devotion, and commitment. I'm so proud of you! Take a moment to acknowledge all you've accomplished. By simply working on clearing your clutter you raised not only your vibration but also the energy of those around you, your community, and the world.

You devoted time to learning, contemplating, and answering questions about clutter in five areas of your life: physical, mental, emotional, spiritual, and energetic. At the end of each chapter you were guided on how to take action. You also may have created an immediate action plan gathered from all five sections. Hopefully, you cleared some clutter and made changes in your life and have begun to share your gifts with the world.

I don't view this book as a "one and done." You might not have completed all the chapters and/or you may have only been able to take action in a few areas. Down the road, you might have very different responses and choose to review chapters or complete a section you hadn't previously. It's been my experience that personal development is a spiral. I may learn a lesson and later absorb more about the same message at a deeper level. I might fall off the wagon and have to revisit a message I'd previously studied. I concentrate on growing, moving forward, and picking myself up when I fall. I urge you to do the same.

You now have the foundation of knowing where you have clutter in your life as well as an action plan for each topic to help you deal with your clutter. If you're unsure how to move forward with your action plan, consider asking a trusted friend or getting professional support. We all need support in our lives, sometimes a little sometimes a lot. I believe when you ask for support the people who can help you show up in your life.

Life is about being in the present moment and that's your point of power to change. Be in the flow of life and open to change and discovery. Trust the process and trust that you're exactly where you need to be.

I'm wishing you much love, happiness, peace, abundance, joy, and laughter.

# Life Inventory Questions

In Chapter 18, *Taking Stock*, I offered some categories and a few questions you may consider as you take a life inventory.

Here's a list of more questions to consider about your life. You don't need to answer all of them. If this is overwhelming, just answer a few. The goal here is to get you thinking, becoming more aware, and being open to change and possibilities. You can't change what you don't acknowledge. Be honest, but have compassion for yourself. Accept yourself and be kind no matter what your answers.

- How well do I allow myself to feel?
- Am I generally happy or sad?
- Do I honor my emotions or do I explode and/or push them down?
- Do I use another poor habit (shopping, overeating) to compensate?
- Do I feel free or trapped? Generally at peace or stressed out?
- Am I open or close-minded?
- What are my bad habits?
- Am I able to stay focused and achieve my goals?
- Do I like my career or do I have a job that just pays the bills?
- Am I fulfilled in most areas of my life the majority of the time?
- Where in life do I lose my integrity by doing acts I don't want to, or aren't comfortable, doing?
- When, or where do I usually, procrastinate?
- Do I mainly live with happiness, joy, and love or

sadness, anger, and fear?
- Am I holding on to past hurts, or have I healed and moved forward?
- Am I anxious about the future? Or am I able to do something when I'm concerned about what can happen?
- How often am I truly in the present moment?
- How have my fears or doubts held me back?
- Do I gossip?
- How well do I take care of my mental state?
- Do I have a mindfulness practice?
- What life lessons have I learned?
- Do I have healthy, happy and balanced relationships, or ones with drama, disappointment and pain?
- Is my life balanced or does one area (health, work) seem to dominate?
- Do I forgive or hold on to resentments?
- Am I jealous or do I celebrate the success of others?
- How well do I handle stress?
- Do I honor myself or do things just because they've always been done that way?
- Am I aware of my weaknesses and work to improve?
- Am I judgmental towards myself and others or do I have compassion?
- Am I generally trusting or fearful?
- Do I take care of myself or do I have unhealthy habits?
- Do I like what I see when I look in the mirror?
- Am I able to budget my time, energy, money, and resources?

- Am I able to set boundaries and say no, or do I let people take advantage of me?
- How kind am I to myself and others?
- Do I feel healthy and fit or sick and tired?
- How well do I love?
- Am I striving for my dreams or passively living life?
- Do I have gratitude or take life and all I have for granted?
- Am I able to unplug and take breaks from social media or do I need to be connected all the time?
- Do I balance my online time with "in real life" time?
- How well am I connected to other people and my community?
- Do I give back or believe in scarcity and hold onto money and possessions?
- Do I like and love myself? Am I indifferent to myself or hate myself?
- Do I take personal responsibility or blame others?
- Do I own my personal power or see myself as a victim? Do I get my needs met in healthy or unhealthy ways?
- Am I living up to my potential?
- When live throws me a challenge how do I respond? Do I become paralyzed and stay stuck, or do I move forward?
- Am I living my passion, mission, or purpose?
- What is my relationship to God, a Higher Power, or the Universe?

# ENDNOTES

1. When I let go of someone from my life, I also let go of the wedding gift she gave me. Every time I saw the gift it would remind me of her and some unpleasant things that had transpired. When I released it, I was free.

2. https://www.telegraph.co.uk/science/2017/12/05/many-toys-bad-children-study-suggests/

3. I met Peter when I won an award in 2011 in Los Angeles. He was gracious, kind, and let me interview him later for my online Internet T.V. show. His episode is still my most popular video on YouTube.

4. http://www.thesharespace.com/BlogPostDetail/?entryId=230

5. I need to study this. Why do we put a pen back in the drawer we can't use? I've been guilty of it as if somehow the pen fairy will fix it.

6. I have to give a shout out to my Aunt Sue. One Christmas the Steelers were playing and a few of us watched the game during dinner. Trust me, this was a big deal. Aunt Sue was probably concerned, like I am, about my grandmother reaching down from heaven. If anyone can come back from heaven to reprimand us, it's my grandmother!

7. Just to confirm that the Universe had my back, my iPad lost its battery soon after our conversation. In an uncomedy of errors, I was without my iPad for two weeks. This was a good first step in real unplugging from social media.

8. https://www.nytimes.com/2017/01/09/well/live/hooked-on-our-smartphones.html

9. https://www.pcmag.com/article/361587/tech-addiction-by-the-numbers-how-much-time-we-spend-online.

10. https://munews.missouri.edu/news-releases/2015/0203-if-facebook-use-causes-envy-depression-could-follow/

11. https://www.nytimes.com/2007/07/25/health/25iht-fat.4.6830240.html

12. Once I removed my height requirement, I met my husband two weeks later. He's shorter than I am. You gotta love the Universe's sense of humor!

13. Be mindful of how many people with whom you share your story and feelings. It's easy to fall into the trap of retelling your experience to many people. If you choose wisely, you'll receive a lot of support. You can get stuck in repeating the event so many times making that the focus instead of using your experience as a jumping-off point for self care, healing, and going onward and upward.

14. https://thebiglead.com/2016/02/18/monty-williams-gives-stirring-eulogy-for-wife-ingrid-urges-forgiveness-for-other-driver/

15. https://food.allwomenstalk.com/kitchen-gadgets-everyone-has-but-never-uses

16. https://theweek.com/articles/484520/3-billion-celebrity-gossip-industry-by-numbers

17.http://iml.jou.ufl.edu/projects/fall04/fernandez/stats.html

18. https://www.psychologytoday.com/intl/blog/the-friendship-doctor/200911/resisting-the-urge-gossip

19. I'll save the discussion as to why girls who sleep with multiple partners are labeled "sluts" and men who do the same are "studs" for another time.

20. I thought this article summed it up nicely. https://www.learning-mind.com/everything-is-energy/

21. I am taking a online plant medicine course, A Year of Gaia. https://www.gaiaschoolofhealing.com/yearofgaia. Please don't use the term smudging. Also look for ethically and sustainably harvested materials. White Sage, Palo Santo, Frankincense, desert Artemsias are threatened species, so please don't buy.

# YOUR FREE GIFT

Free MP3 Meditation to release clutter. Choose: physical, mental, emotional, spiritual or energetic. Send an email to Julie@reawakenyourbrilliance.com with your selection.

# RESOURCES

Clear Your Clutter Inside & Out Podcast:
https://itunes.apple.com/us/podcast/clearing-clutter-inside-out/id914959979

Clear Your Clutter Inside & Out Videos:
https://www.youtube.com/user/SeibertRadio?feature=watch

# BOOKS & CLASSES

https://reawakenyourbrilliance.com/shop/

# LET'S CONNECT

Facebook: https://www.facebook.com/ReawakenYourBrilliance

Twitter: https://twitter.com/ReawakeBrillian

Instagram: https://www.instagram.com/reawakenyourbrilliance/

Linked In: https://www.linkedin.com/in/juliescoraccio

Tumblr: https://www.tumblr.com/blog/reawakenyourbrilliance

## Need a more tailored approach to declutter your life?

Learn how Julie can support you in coaching, customized classes, professional speaking, online workshops, & more.
http://reawakenyourbrilliance.com

# GRATITUDES

*I'm so very grateful and consciously choose to use the word gratitude because acknowledging these wonderful people didn't seem to fully capture how appreciative I am. As I practice gratitude daily, and encourage others to do so, this phrasing made the most sense for me.*

Tony, I could not have completed this book without your support. Thanks for believing in me when I couldn't believe in myself.

Joey, thanks for having daily snuggy time with momma. Antonio, you make me smile everyday, and Athena, thank you for reminding me I can be a warrior and a goddess simultaneously. Annina and Augusta, I didn't save either of you; you both saved me.

To Lisa Transcendence Brown, Judy Nelson, A. Kimball Pike, Mardi Wasserman, and all the other teachers along my path who have supported me in clearing my own clutter.

Kaadi Taylor, thank you for so many years of deep and supportive friendship. It takes a brave and true friend to look at a very rough first draft! Your feedback for this book took it to the next level. I'm up for continuing care packages for critiques if you are.

James Seibert (Big J) who always believes in me and told me he would support me as long as I didn't do anything "illegal, immoral or unethical." So far, so good. Thank you for always being in my corner and welcoming Tony into our family.

Jenny Seibert (Jen Jen) for all the adventures you've given me in life and getting me out into the bigger world. And most importantly for editing this book in the early stages and doing the final grammar check. Thank you for treating Tony like a son.

For my niece Emma for being fierce, fabulous, and funny, and creating Varuit. You are beautiful and make me laugh every time I see you.

My funny, handsome, and soccer-playing nephew Max for reminding me that each day is the best day ever and it's okay to be lovingly teased. I will beat you at bridge.

For my smart, creative, and talented niece Clare, my favorite triple threat and fellow lover of baking, I enjoy watching you bloom into a lovely young woman.

My uncle, author, and Hosta aficionado, Jim Henry, for kicking my butt in grammar edits, sharing the joy of hostas, bringing valuable insights, and having the best partner, Herb Burgess, who smiles through life.

Stephanie Hannus for the brilliant cover design. Seeing the book cover come to life kept me going as I slogged through edits.

My teachers: Julie Squibb for keeping my junior high "horror" story for years; Loretta Thompson who honored me with a King Arthur Author Award in junior high; Karen Moore who taught me in high school how to research and write a quality paper; and Professor Anthony Farnham who awarded me a Merrill Prize for English my freshman year in college and saw creativity despite my grammatical challenges.

To my clients: You inspire me with your willingness to go deep and take risks. It's a lot easier to remain unaware, so Bravo and Brava!

The listeners and viewers of *Clear Your Clutter Inside & Out*: thanks for tuning in, all your kind words, and letting me know how much the episodes mean to you.

For the readers undertaking the journey of this book: The world needs your gifts, so thank you for taking the first step to declutter your life. I'm cheering you up that spiral.

Julie Coraccio lives in Raleigh, NC, with her husband Tony and their rescued black cats Joey and Antonio, brown tabby Athena, and tuxedos Annina and Augusta. A native West Virginian, she is passionate about supporting people in clearing clutter in all areas of their lives, end of life organization, and helping them becoming more mindful and aware. Julie is a graduate of Mount Holyoke College and hosts the weekly podcast *Clear Your Clutter Inside & Out.* She enjoys hiking, cooking and baking, alternative medicine and healing, supporting environmental and animal causes, and enjoying her woman cave—a bubble bath. Julie is the author of the journal prompts series *Got Clutter? 365 Journal Prompts.* Find her free podcast at ReawakenYourBrilliance.com

Made in the USA
Coppell, TX
08 September 2021